COMMON EDIBLE AND USEFUL
PLANTS OF THE WEST

By Muriel Sweet

Edited by Vinson Brown

Major Illustrators
Emily Reid, Charles Yocom and Barbara Johnson

DEDICATED TO

My husband, Nathan Sweet, whose encouragement
kept me going until the finish, and
Charles Horn, whose help and fine criticism made
this possible.

COLOR PICTURES ON COVER
Left: Butterfly Mariposa Lily   Right: Wild Rose
Photos by and courtesy of E. F. Jewett

Copyright 1962, by Muriel Sweet

Paper Edition   ISBN 0-911010-54-8
Cloth Edition   ISBN 0-911010-55-6

Published by Naturegraph Company, Healdsburg, California

TABLE OF CONTENTS

Southern Goldenrod

"To win the secrets of a weed's plain heart."

James Russell Lowell

INTRODUCTION

It is my hope that this small volume may prove to be of use to many who are interested in a short history, in non-technical language, of some western plants, and of their uses by the Indians and others as food as well as medicine. To describe all the useful and edible plants of the west would take a volume many times this size, but described here are those I consider most important or interesting and certainly these would be those, in most cases, most often encountered.

Since some plants of the west are poisonous, it is necessary to be sure of your identification before using a plant for food and several plants must be carefully processed (such as by leaching) before they are edible. The following rules are suggested:

1. Study carefully the descriptions and pictures of the plants in this book to make sure of your identification of each species.

2. Poisonous plants are marked POISONOUS in capitals. Avoid eating these plants. The most dangerous are described on pages 47 and 54. Others less poisonous are on pages 14, 31, 35, 38-9, 40-1, 43, 44, 50, 54, 56, 57, and 58.

3. If any plant has to be specially prepared before eating, follow the directions for preparation very carefully, omitting no details, and being overly careful if anything.

4. A plant with an acrid, bitter or pungent taste may be poisonous and should be left alone unless full details are given as to how to use it. Avoid all mushrooms unless you are an expert.

To aid you in identification the plants are split into easily understood divisions. Water plants, ferns and their allies are lumped together in one group, trees in another, shrubs in a third, herbs in a fourth, and vines in a fifth. At the start of the larger sections plants are also divided by color of flower. To conserve space the habitats or living places of plants are given the following easily recognized abbreviations which are placed along the margins, as are also the names of states where they are found.

Des. = desert scrub; PJ = pinyon-juniper woodland; Oak = oak woodland; Sage = sagebrush scrub; Chap. = chaparral or brush; CCF = coastal coniferous forest; MCF = mountain coniferous forest; SA = sub-alpine forest; Alp. = alpine fell fields; SW = streamside woodland; Gr. = grassland; Md. - meadows; Msh = marshlands; Wtr. = ponds, streams, etc.; Clt. = cultivated or otherwise disturbed areas.

WATER PLANTS AND FERNS AND
THEIR ALLIES

W-1. BRACKEN FERN,
<u>Pteridium aquilinum</u>; Fern
Fam. 1'-4' high. Distinc-
tive, dark, cord-like, root-
stocks; lower pinnules of
leaf toothed, upper smooth.

The root is viscid, bit-
terish and, like most of
the fern tribe, has a salty

Wtr. and mucilaginous taste.
Msh When burned, the ashes
Md.
SW yield more salt than other
vegetables. Also good as

Most fertilizer for potatoes if
Sts.,
W. worked into the ground.
Can.   The astringency is so great that it is used abroad in preparing
chamois leather. In Siberia and other northern countries, the in-
habitants brew the roots in their ale, mixing one-third of roots with
two-thirds of malt. Ancients used the roots and whole plant in de-
coctions and diet drinks for the spleen and other disorders. Japa-
nese use it in soup. Indians boiled and ate the root stocks, as they
are starchy; also used them as a diuretic and worm medicine. In
early days the tops were used in the spring, while still curled, as
asparagus. Pioneers would soak them in water with wood ashes for
24 hours, then cook the young leaves like pot herbs. The fern was
also used in a decoction as a cure for rickets in children.

W-2. HORSETAIL or SCOURING RUSH, <u>Equi-</u>
<u>setum arvense</u>; Horsetail Fam. Eaten by Romans
in 17th century, the young heads were boiled like

Oak asparagus, or mixed with flour and fried. Indians
SW and early settlers used the stems as a stimulat-
CCF
MCF ing diuretic in kidney and dropsical disorders.
      The outer layer of the stems contains a quan-
Most tity of silica useful in polishing hardwood, ivory
Sts.,
W. and brass; also used by Mexicans and Indians for scouring pots.
Can.   Aconitic acid in plant is poisonous to horses but not to cows or
goats. Bears and muskrats eat it and rootstocks eaten by geese.

W-3. CATTAIL, Typha sp, ; Cattail Fam.
3'-7' tall, with very long, slender leaves and
typical sausage shaped catkins, forming feathery tips with age.

The Greek, Dioscorides wrote: "the starchy substance mixed with axungia (hog or goose
grease) is good to heal burnings, it doth moderately cleanse and dry, and being applied to
bleeding places stancheth blood."

Our Indians made much use of the leaves
for chairs and mats. In winter leading shoots
of root stock are filled with starchy material
and are used as a salad or cooked as a vegetable. Root stocks are also dried and ground
into meal, being equal in food value to rice or
corn. The people of Bombay, India, harvest
the pollen and make bread from it. Young
flowering shoots, before pollen has developed,
are eaten either raw or boiled and considered
a great delicacy.

Wtr.
Msh

Most
Sts.,
W.
Can.

Root stocks are more valuable than seed as food for wild life.
Geese and muskrats eat the starchy underground stems. The
plants form nesting shelters for many marsh birds.

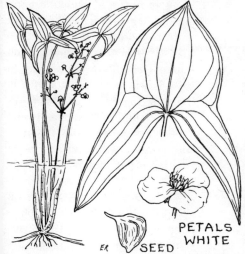

PETALS WHITE
SEED

W-4. ARROWHEAD or
TULE POTATO, Sagittaria
sp.; Water Plantain Fam.
About 3' high, with flowers
growing around stem in
whorls of 3, and leaves
sheathing stem at base.
Fibrous roots and milky
juice. Grows in meadows
up to 6000'.

Wtr.
Msh

Most
Sts.,
W.
Can.

When Lewis and Clark
were camped in Oregon,
they practically lived on
the tubers purchased from
the Indians. The tubers are
found several feet away from the plant.   Muskrats store them in
their nests, where the Indians would gather them.   After boiling,

the Indians sliced them and strung them up for winter use, calling them Wapato. The Chinese in California used the tubers roasted or boiled. Large tubers, 2 inches in diameter, contain a milky juice when raw that is quite unpleasant, but very sweet when roasted. In England corms are ground fine and yield a flour that can be used in making cookies, muffins or puddings.

W-5. WATERCRESS, Nasturtium officinale; Mustard Fam. The prostrate or ascending stems grow from wet places or in water; small white flowers in racemes, Naturalized from Europe.

Wtr. Msh

Most Sts., W. Can.

Xenophon recommended it to the Persians to make children strong and it was much prized by the Moslems. Romans considered it excellent food for people with deranged minds.

Wtr. Msh

Parkinson in 1640 says,

Most Sts. W. Can.

"Leaves or juice applied to the face or other parts troubled with freckles, pimples, spots or the like, at night and washed away in the morning. The juice mixed with vinegar to the forehead is good for lethargy or drowsy feeling!'

Coronado found it near the Gila River in Arizona and in 1769 Padre Crespi speaks of it. In 1806 Lewis and Clark found it in Oregon. Indians used the plant for liver and kidney trouble and to dissolve gallstones. It is now commonly used for salads and to garnish other dishes.

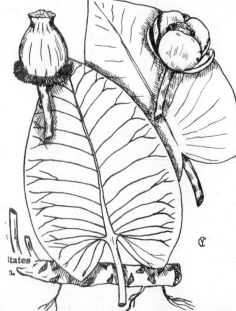

W-6. INDIAN POND LILY or YELLOW WATER LILY, Nuphar polysepalum; Water-lily Fam. Large leaves rise from thick rootstock. Rootstocks baked; seeds for bread and soups.

V-1. WESTERN VIRGIN'S BOWER, Clematis ligusticifolia; Buttercup Fam. Climbs by aid of the petioles of the opposite and compound leaves; flowers with white, petal-like sepals, but no petals; leaflets 5-7; flowers turn into feather-like seeds. Called Yerba de Chivato, "herb of the goat" by Spanish-Americans who used it to wash wounds.

SW
Oak
CCF
MCF

Most
Sts.,
W.
Can.

Indians used white portion of bark for fever, leaves and bark for shampoo, and a decoction of the leaves was used on horses for sores and cuts. From fibers they made snares and carrying nets. Pharmocopia says it is useful in treatment of skin diseases, ulcers, colds and many eruptions. In 16th century doctors used it internally in powdered form to cure bone pains.

V-2. COMMON GOURD, Curcurbita foetidissima; Gourd Fam. A creeping vine, with coarse, hairy leaves, fairly large, yellow flowers and green-striped fruit balls. Called Calabazilla by Spanish Californians and Chili Coyote by Mexicans.

Indians crushed roots and pith of fruit for soap to wash clothes, but were careful to rinse several times due to prickly hairs. The seeds, ground, were eaten and portions of the gourd made a strong purge, though an overdose can prove fatal. They made a

Oak
Gr.
Sage
Des.

Most
Sts.

tea for bloat in horses and also for worms.   The top of the plant
was supposed to cure ailments of the head and roots of the feet.

Indians along the Rio Grande would grind roots and mix with
water as a laxative.   Navajos used dried gourds as rattles   in
their dances. <u>Pharmacopia</u> says, "pulp of green fruit mixed with
soap applied to ulcers and sores; leaves used medicinally. "

V-3, WILD CUCUMBER
<u>Marah</u> sp.   Also called
Manroot and Big Root
Chilicote. A trailing or
climbing vine,with ivylike,
SW
Oak   thin leaves;.flowers small,
              greenish-white;   large,
Was.   green, prickly seed pods.
Ore.
Cal.   When pods are ripe, they
W.   pop open and scatter large
Can.   brown seeds covered with
              a soapy pulp.

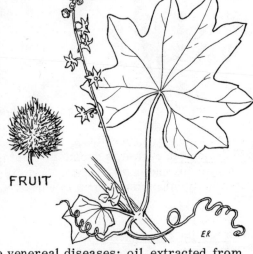

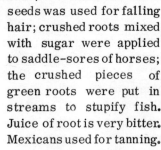

FRUIT

The Indians roasted the
seeds and ate them   for
kidney trouble. Decoction
of plant was drunk to cure venereal diseases; oil extracted from
seeds was used for falling
hair; crushed roots mixed
with sugar were applied
to saddle-sores of horses;
the crushed pieces   of
green roots were put in
streams to stupify fish.
Juice of root is very bitter.
Mexicans used for tanning.

V-4,   WILD GRAPE,
<u>Vitis</u> <u>californica</u>; Grape
Fam. 5'-60' long vine with
clusters of small, green-
ish or white flowers.

SW
Oak

Ore.   FRUIT
Cal.   PURPLE

Grapes are edible and
good thirst quenchers. Used for jellies, preserves   and drinks.

PINES, <u>Pinus</u> sp.; Pine Fam. Noted for their slender needles in bunches and large cones, all produce pine nuts in the cones that are edible, but the following species especially so:

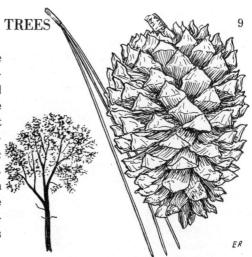

T-1. Digger Pine, <u>P. Sabiniana</u>. 3 needles in bunch; a scraggly tree growing in the lower altitudes of most mountains of California along the Pacific Coast. The soft center of the green cones, roasted for about 20 minutes in hot ashes, yields a sort of syrupy food that was MCF much relished by the Indians. Seeds are rich in fat and proteins Cal. and usually eaten raw. Yellow pitch from the tree is a protective counter-irritant. Bark infusion reputed useful for consumption. Twigs and leaves used in decoction for rheumatism. Twigs and rootlets used as sewing material for baskets. Charcoal from nut meats crushed and applied to sores and burns.

One-leaved Pinyon Pine

T-2. Two-leaved Pinyon Pine, <u>P. edulis</u>, and One-Leaved Pinyon Pine, <u>P. monophylla</u>, are both desert mountain trees with short needles and MCF small cones. Seeds are Ut. rich in protein and used as Nev. food by Indians. The nuts Cal. were pounded and made Ar. into cakes or cooked as a gruel. Cones were picked before they fell and put on a fire to loosen the nuts or seeds. Often a soup was made from the nuts to give to babies.

T-3. Sugar Pine, <u>Pinus</u> <u>Lambertiana</u>. Very tall tree, with thick foliage; needles in bunches of 5's; large, long cones; sweetish sap.

MCF
CCF

Ore.
Cal.

The sap yields a saccharine that is very sweet, but acts as a cathartic if very much eaten. Powdered resin was used by the Indians for sores and ulcers. The hardened sap was dissolved and used to wash sore eyes; pitch was used to mend canoes, to fasten arrowheads and feathers. Nuts and shells were pulverized until like butter, then eaten or put into soup.

MCF

Most
Sts.
W.
Can.

T-4. Western Yellow Pine, <u>P</u>. <u>ponderosa</u>. Tall pine with 3 long needles in bunch, bark on older trees yellowish and picture-puzzle-like, smelling of vanilla. The gummy pitch from the bark is very adhesive and was used by the Indians for canoes and on tents. The mistletoe that grows on this pine was used in a decoction as a stomach aid and to relieve colic.

CCF
MCF

Most
Sts.
W.
Can.

T-5. Lodgepole Pine, <u>P</u>. <u>contorta</u>. Usually has straight trunk, but scraggly branches; needles in 2's and 1 1/2"-2 3/4" long. The buds were chewed by the Indians for sore throat and pitch was put on open sores. The inner bark was mashed into a pulp and made into cakes. These cakes were put between skunk cabbage leaves, a fire of wet material was made on top of them, and they were left to bake for an hour or more. Then they were smoked and put away after being pressed into firmness to be used on trips.

Lodgepole
Pine

MCF

Most
Sts.
W.
Can.

White
Pine

T-6. Western White Pine, <u>P</u>. <u>monticola</u>. Also called Silver Pine. Bark whitish or reddish and smooth; needles in 5's and very slender, 2"-4" long; 6"-10" long cones are very slender when closed, and green or dark purple when young. The young shoots were boiled by the Indians and used for rheumatism, kidney trouble, boils and coughs. Bark was boiled and decoction made for stomach disorders. The pitch was used to fasten feathers to arrow shafts; also was rubbed on the shafts to make them stronger and more elastic.

The young, inner bark of most pines could be used for food in cases of starvation by thoroughly pounding.

T-7. CALIFORNIA FAN PALM, <u>Washingtonia</u> <u>fili-fera</u>; Palm Fam. These palms grow in moist alkaline soil below 3500' and are 20'-75' tall, with leaves 3'-6' long, torn almost to the middle, making a ragged appearance. From the long fibrous strings the fruiting branches hang 8 to 21' in large clusters of berries that sway in the wind.

Des.
SW

Cal.

Berries turn black when ripe and are eagerly eaten by birds and animals. Orioles use the threads from the leaves for nests.

The Indians would roast and eat the berries; also grind them into flour for cakes. Strings from the leaves were used in basket weaving. They would sometimes cut the terminal bud to roast and eat as a great delicacy, but this would cause the tree to die. Leaves were used to thatch their houses and the trunks were sometimes used as building timber.

T-8. JOSHUA TREE, <u>Yucca</u> <u>brevifolia</u>; Lily Fam. A long-armed, scraggly tree, 16'-30' high, usually growing in high deserts of around 3000'-4500' altitude. The dark brown bark is marked off into small square plates; narrow sharp leaves 6-9" long; greenish-white flowers in thick panicle, 8"-14" long.

POD

FLOWER

JC

Des.
PJ

Ut.
Ar.
Cal.
Nev.

The Indians made a red dye from the red rootlets, which were also used for weaving patterns in baskets. The flower buds were eaten hot or cold after roasting. They were sweet because of high sugar content and were often given as

LEAF

candy to the children. The pioneers used the wood for fence posts.

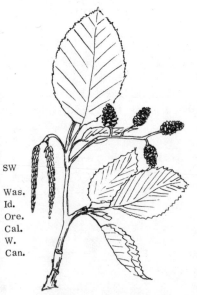

SW

Was.
Id.
Ore.
Cal.
W.
Can.

T-9. WHITE ALDER, Alnus rhombifolia, Birch Fam. Also other species of Alnus. A tree 15'-30' high, with light green leaves, whitish to gray bark, green hanging catkins, and small, brown, 2"-4" long cones; very common along streams.

Parkinson, in 1640, writes of Alnus: "Leaves and bark are cooling and drying. Fresh leaves laid on tumors will dissolve them; also stays inflammation. Leaves with morning dew on them; laid on a floor troubled with fleas, will gather the fleas and can then be quickly thrown out. A black dye was made from the bark."

Indians used a decoction of dried bark to induce circulation, check diarrhea, allay stomach-ache, facilitate childbirth, check hemorrhages, and, mixed with Indian tobacco, to induce vomiting. They also made a dye that was yellow-brown. Early settlers made charcoal and used it in the preparation of inferior gunpowder. The astringent bark and woody cones were used for tanning leather. For dye, the bark was peeled in the spring.

T-10. OAKS, Quercus sp., Beech Fam. The oaks form a large genus of about 200 species. Acorns of the Black Oak (Q. kellogii), and the Blue Oak (Q. douglasii) seem to be the favorites though several others were used by the Indians. However, they were careful to keep different kinds of acorns separate.

Oak
SW

Ore.
Cal.
Ar.

The acorns were soaked overnight to make it easier to get the kernels from the outer shell. After they were shelled and dried, the meats were

Blue Oak
ER

ground into a flour or meal. If possible, the
meal was put in a sand hollow, and covered with
twigs of Douglas Fir, Cedar or White Fir to break
the force of the water poured over to leach the
meal (a sieve could be used in place of sand). This
was done about ten times. To remove the meal,
the hand was pressed on it and the adhering meal

Black Oak   ER

put in a basket. Any sand that was in the meal was washed out by
pouring water through the basket. Hot stones were used in cooking meal. Often meal was leached through cedar twigs for flavor.

Soup, bread and a pudding were made from the meal or flour.
One kind of bread was made by wrapping the dough in fern leaves
and baking in hot ashes. Leavened bread was made from the Water Oak (Quercus nigra) of eastern Texas and many southeastern
states. A small amount of ashes was added to the dough,   which
made the bread rise. It was baked in an earth oven.

Sometimes acorn meal was allowed to accumulate a mold. The
mold was scraped off, kept in a damp place, and used to heal boils,
sores and other inflamations.

T-11. CALIFORNIA BAY
TREE, OREGON MYRTLE or
CALIFORNIA LAUREL, Um-
bellularia californica. Laurel
Fam. 50'-100' high tree, with
dark green leaves that have a
strong,   pungent odor when
crushed; small greenish-yel-
low flowers in clusters of 6-10;
solitary fruits turn dark purple.   Shaded areas.

The wood is yellow-brown,
takes a high polish, and is used
for furniture, boat building, etc.
Indians wore a leaf under their
hats to cure a headache.   The
fruit was roasted and eaten.

Crushed leaves, when held
near the nose, will produce se-
vere   headache or sneezing.

SW
Oak

Ore.
Cal.

Both leaves and seeds contain an oil reputed to have anesthetic

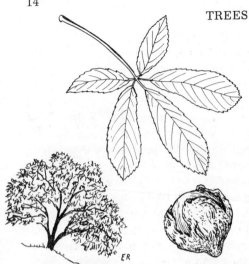

properties. Also useful in nervous disorders, intestinal colic, and as an insecticide (said to drive away fleas and lice). The small limbs are used today on chicken roosts as a louse preventitive. The leaves are good flavor additives to stews, roasts, etc. Hung up with garlic to dry, they prevent molding.

T-12. CALIFORNIA BUCKEYE, Aesculus californica; Buckeye Fam. 12'-25' high tree, with 5 finger-like, light green leaflets to each leaf; beautiful white flowers in candle-stick-like spikes, turning into round, brown balls in the fruit; leaves turn bronze in August. Grows in California up to 3000' altitude.

SW
Oak

Cal.

While the flowers are bad for bees, and the leaves eaten by cows produce poor-flavored milk, the tree is useful otherwise. Unripe seeds were crushed and scattered into streams to stupify the fish. Ripe seeds can be crushed and leached, after roasting which takes out most of the poison. Water must be poured over the ground meal at least ten times, but the best leaching is done by letting water in a small stream run over the meal for ten days. The meal is then cooked as a pudding.

Leaves were steeped to make a tea as a remedy for congestion of the lungs and varicose veins. Seeds were buried in swampy, cold ground during the winter to free them of bitter quality, and eaten in the spring boiled. The wood was used for fire-making.

SW
Oak

Cal.

T-13. CALIFORNIA WALNUT, Juglans californica. Walnut Fam. 15'-35' high tree or shrub; dark bark; 9-17 leaflets.

The brown nuts are edible.

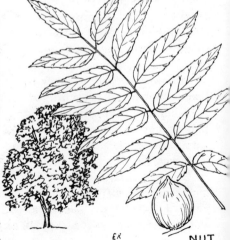

NUT

SHRUBS

The colors of flowers, fruits, seeds, etc. that are given on this page should be used in the field to help you with quick identification of the species you encounter, but should not be used alone. Carefully study the descriptions and pictures of all species before making up your mind that you have made correct identifications.

FLOWER COLORS

White, whitish or cream: 2, 3, 6, 7, 8, 9, 10, 11, 12, 13, 15, 17, 22, 24, 26, 27, 28, 29, 20, 21, 32, 33.

Greenish: 1, 2, 4, 8, 20, 21, 23.

Purple, violet, lavender: 2, 8, 17, 18, 24, 26, 28, 31.

Red, reddish-brown or pink: 2, 3, 8, 13, 14, 15, 17, 22, 24, 27, 30, 31, 33.

Yellow: 5, 16, 17, 19, 20, 22, 23, 25, 29, 30, 31, 33.

Blue or bluish: 17, 24, 27, 28, 29, 31.

FRUIT AND SEED COLORS
(Not all fruits and seeds are listed here.)

B = berries; F = fruits; N = nutlets; P = pods; S = seeds.

Green or greenish: 1 (S), 15 (P), 22 (S), 24 (B).

Black or purplish-black: 2 (S), 5 (B), 11 (B), 12 (B), 23 (B), 28 (S).

Brown or brownish: 3 (F), 4 (B), 7 (F), 11 (B and S), 16 (S), 17 (P), 20 (N), 24 (S), 25 (S), 28 (B), 29 (N).

Gray or grayish: 5 (B), 6 (F), 25 (S).

Blue: 5 (B), 32 (B).

Yellow or orange: 5 (B), 15 (B), 30 (S).

Red, pink or reddish: 5 (B), 9 (F), 10 (F), 13 (B), 14 (B), 15 (B and S), 21 (B), 22 (B), 26 (B), 27 (B).

Purple or violet: 5 (B), 11 (B), 14 (P).

White or whitish: 19 (F), 24 (B), 33 (B).

S-1.   EPHEDRA, JOINT FIR, MORMON TEA,
Ephedra californica; Ephedra Fam. 1-2' high, and
with long, jointed stems; opposite and scale-like
leaves; slender stalks often broom-like and green.

Des.   Ancient medicinal plant, used by the father of
PJ   Chinese Medicine, Shen Mung, in 2698 B.C. Dried
Chap. roots and stems;used in treatment of coughs, for
Gr.   colds, headache and fever. Stems sold in Chinese
Cal.   stores under name Ma-Huang. Chinese variety
       is what the alkaloid ephedrin is made from;   our
       variety has a high percentage of tannin.

It was a beverage for Indians as well as roasted and ground for bitter bread. One tribe made a
decoction of the entire plant and drank it to help
stop bleeding. Pioneers made a tea used as a blood purifier. The
deer and sheep eat bark and foliage, if food scarce. Quail eat seed.

FLOWER CONE

FRUIT CONE

S-2.   YUCCAS, AMOLES,
Yucca sp.; Lily Fam. 2-18' high
Des.   with thickly-clustered, sharply-
Chap. pointed leaves; large,   whitish
Cal.   flowers form, towering, termi-
Ar.   nal panicles; black seeds. The
N. M. flowers are   pollinated by the
Col.   night-flying Pronuba moth.

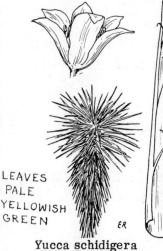

LEAVES
PALE
YELLOWISH
GREEN

ER

LEAF

4'-16'   ER

Fleshy-fruited Yucca, Y. baccat

Yucca schidigera

Indians eat the flowers.   The stalks
are rich in sugar; the leaves produce a
fibre used in making baskets and mats.
The roots are used as a substitute for
soap and for cleaning hair.   The large,
pulpy fruits of Y. baccata are eaten raw,
roasted, or cooked and dried for future
use. Cattle eat the flowers.

S-3. BUCKWHEAT, BUSH, <u>Eriogonum fas-ciculatum</u>. Buckwheat Fam. Similar to several other buckwheat shrubs. but this species has shreddy bark. 2-3' high, with woody base; the numerous leaves densely-white-woolly beneath, green above, and smooth.

Uses of Buckwheat are described on page 37 under H-9.

FLOWERS PINKISH WHITE

Chap.
Des.
Sage
PJ
MCF

Cal.
Nev.
Ar.

2-3'
ER

S-4. SHADSCALE SALTBUSH, <u>Atriplex canescens</u>. Saltbush Fam. A roundish and gray bush, 1-5' high, with flowers in narrow spike-like panicles, gray to dull green; the leaves covered with tiny white hairs and bran-like scales; fruit bracts are toothed as shown on the wings (in illus.). Bushes often cover vast areas, or are associated with creosote and sage brush, generally in moderately saline dry soil.

Cal.
Ar.
Nev.
N. M.

Des.
Chap.
PJ

Indians ground seed for meal and also used them as an emetic. Leaves sometimes eaten as spinach. Zuni Indians in New Mexico ground roots and blossoms moistened with saliva to use for ant bites. Also stirred ashes of Saltbush into batter of their water bread in order to change color of meal to greenish-blue. White New Mexicans chew green leaves with a pinch of salt to relieve bad stomach pains.

CCF
MCF
Chap.

Shadscale has high forage value due to the nutritive quality and evergreen habit, also richness of the seeds in sodium and other salts. Deer eat twigs and foliage; ground squirrels, rabbits and kangaroo rats eat seeds and leaves.

Most
Sts.
W.
Can.

S-5. BARBERRY and MOUNTAIN GRAPE, <u>Berberis</u> sp. (see illustration on next page); Sweetshrub Fam. An erect-growing shrub, with holly-like leaves, fragrant yellow flowers in racemes, followed by bluish berries, and growing from sea level to 5000'

altitude; most are bushes, but B. repens
(Creeping Barberry) crawls low over
ground. All are lovely garden shrubs
with bronze-crimson, autumn leaves.
The wood is of a beautiful yellow color,
used by Spanish-Americans to make
neck crosses (crucifixes).

Juice of the fruit fermented with sugar makes an excellent wine; also a jelly
made from the juice is very tart but
very good served with meat.   Berries
boiled in soup add flavor. Indians used
roots and bark for ulcers, sores and
as a tonic, also in a decoction for consumption, heartburn and rheumatism.
Bark and roots are made into a yellow dye. Leaves are chewed
for acne. Liquid from chewed root was placed on injuries and on
wounds, while cuts and bruises were washed with a root decoction.
Root tea was used as blood tonic, cough medicine, and for kidneys.

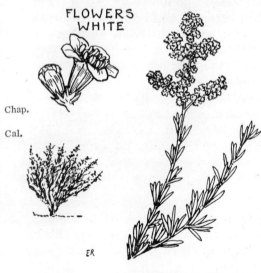

FLOWERS
WHITE

Chap.

Cal.

ER

S-6. CHAMISE, Adenos-
toma fasciculatum;   Rose
Fam. A spreading   shrub,
2'-10' high, with slender,
wand-like branches and
graceful, pyramidal clusters of white flowers in
June; fruits gray; new bark
is reddish, turning gray
when old. It is quick to catch
fire due to resin in leaves.
If burned, the first year's
leaves are grazed by stock
and deer. Bees frequent the
blossoms for pollen; gold-
finches and woodrats eat the
seeds.

Indians used an infusion of bark and leaves as a cure for syphilis; also an oil yielded by the plant was used for skin infections.
Sick cows find benefit from the plant by chewing on the leaves.

The wood burns very quickly with a bright flame and supplies
quick heat for cooking.

S-7. BEAR CLOVER or MOUNTAIN MISERY, <u>Chamaebatia</u> <u>foliolosa</u>; Rose Fam. Indian name is <u>Kitkitisu</u>. It is called "Mountain Misery" because of the properties of the leaves that cover all clothing with sticky black gum.

The plant is a low-growing shrub not over 2' high, with small, white, strawberry-like flowers; fruit brown; leaves finely-dissected and fern-like.

Indians used plant for many ailments: leaves were steeped in hot water to make tea used for rheumatism, skin eruptions, etc.; leaves also used in a decoction for coughs and colds. Sometimes used as a medicine to treat venereal diseases. **MCF Cal.**

Flowers and fruit fair forage for deer and stock. Plant fine for erosion purposes due to the mat of roots and closeness of growth, but resinous leaves unfortunately make it a fire hazard.

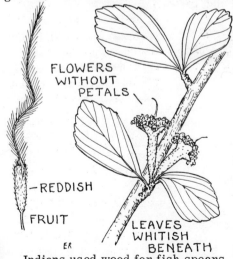

FLOWERS WITHOUT PETALS

—REDDISH

FRUIT

LEAVES WHITISH BENEATH

S-8. MOUNTAIN MAHOGANY, <u>Cercocarpus</u> sp. An evergreen, drought-resistant shrub or low tree; young shoots are reddish-brown, covered with a hairy down; flowers greenish, often turning brownish, whitish or reddish; fruit with a long, feathery, twisted tail giving the bush a silvery look in the sunshine. Rich, dark brown, mahogany-like wood is hard and tough, but also brittle, making hot fire. **Chap. Oak Most Sts.**

Indians used wood for fish spears, arrow shafts and pointed sticks for digging. Inner bark made a purple dye. Bark used in tea to cure colds; also they peeled the bark, scraped the inner layer, then dried and boiled it for lung trouble. The powdered young plant, stirred in water, was used as a laxative.   Spanish-Americans hung branch on bed to discourage bedbugs.

S-9.   CALIFORNIA WILD ROSE, <u>Rosa</u> <u>californica</u>. A scraggly bush, 3-6' high.   Grows along stream and river banks; pretty, light pink flowers, bright red hips (or fruit). Father Font of the Anza Expedition speaks of gathering and eating them right from the bush. Rich in Vitamin A and C.

SW

Ore.
Cal.

FRUIT

FLOWERS WHITE OR PINK

$\times \frac{1}{2}$

ER

Indians made a tea from the tender root shoots for colds; seeds were cooked for muscular pains; leaves and hips steeped and drunk for pains and colics. The old straight wood was used for arrow shafts. Spanish-Californians made jelly from the ripe fruit and ate hips raw from the bush. After the first frost softened the hips, the leaves and petals were astringent and used in perfume. Petals, peppermint, lemon peels and linden leaves made into a tea for arthritis or dyspepsia; petals also said to help dissolve gallstones.

Chap.
MCF
Oak

Most
Sts.

S-10. CHOKECHERRY, <u>Prunus</u> demissa. 3-8' high shrub, with 3-10 white flowers in short clusters; berries bright red or purple.   Extensive thickets.

Inner bark used by Indians as a tonic to check diarrhea and to relieve nervousness. A decoction of young shoots and bark was taken as a vegetable. There were several ways to use the berries. Acid was leached out of fresh berries with water through basket, then they were ground in a stone mortar; the dried pulp was boiled and eaten. Fresh berries were also ground and dried for later use. Berries make a good jelly or jam and wine is sometimes made of them.

There is hydrocyanic acid in the young leaves, which is dangerous for cattle, but it is lost by fall. Animals and birds eat fruit.

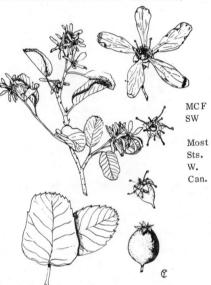

S-11. WESTERN SERVICE BERRY, Amelanchier sp. Also called June Berry. 3-12' high shrub, sometimes a small tree 15'-20' high, growing on dry slopes in mts. or along N. W. coast. Flowers white, fruit purplish-black to brown.

MCF
SW

Most
Sts.
W.
Can.

Europeans made pies and puddings from the berries, always leaving in seeds as they added to the flavor. Indians dried the berries for winter use, also crushed them to make a cake from which they would break off a piece to add to soup or vegetables. They made a sort of pemmican of pounded berries and dried meat with animal fat to be carried on long trips. An eye wash was made from boiled green, inner bark.

CCF
MCF
SW
Oak

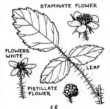

S-12. CALIFORNIA BLACKBERRY, Rubus vitifolius. Stems 1'-8' long, erect as a bush, or trailing over the ground. It is covered with straight, sharp thorns; leaves with double-toothed edges; flower white; edible berries black.

Cal.

Cal.
Ore.
Was.
Id.
W.
Can.

S-13. WESTERN THIMBLE BERRY, Rubus parviflorus. A spreading, 3'-6' high bush; bark becoming shreddy with age; leaves 3"-7" wide, usually with hairy and glandular stems; white or pinkish flowers; the soft, light red berry is sweet and edible.

Oak
CCF
MCF

Most
Sts.

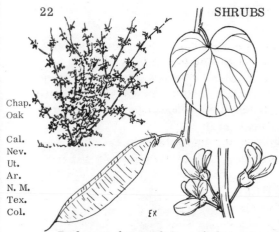

Chap.
Oak

Cal.
Nev.
Ut.
Ar.
N. M.
Tex.
Col.

S-14. REDBUD or JU-DAS TREE, _Cercis_ sp. Pea Fam. Clustered 8'-15' high stems; leaves round, heart-shaped at base; red-purple flowers appear before leaves.

Indians use bark of the young shoots for baskets; medicinally they form a mild astringent in treating diarrhea and dysentery.

Buds can be used in salads or made into pickles. The wood takes a very fine polish.

S-15. CHRISTMAS or TOYON BERRY, _Hetero-meles arbutifolia._ An evergreen shrub, 6-10' high; with simple, serrated leaves; flowers white in small terminal clusters. Grows in the foothills below 4000' altitude.

Oak
Chap.

Cal.

BERRIES RED

x⅓

Early day Californians made a drink from the berries and fishermen in the Channel Islands used the bark to tan their fish nets. Indians boiled the berries and baked them in their ground ovens with hot stones for 2 or 3 days. They also stored berries for a few months, then parched them and made them into meal.

FRUIT PODS

x¼

x½

Des.

Cal.
Nev.
Ar.
N. M.
Tex.

S-16. MESQUITE, _Pro-sopsis_ sp. Large shrub or small tree, 10-35' high, with fern-like leaves and yellow flowers in slender spikes. Will grow below 3000' in mountains.

Indians mixed gum from bark with mud to kill lice; a blue stain
is made to paint the face; fruit or pods are pounded with seeds
and eaten or mixed with water for a sweet drink. Pods and seeds
made into meal are eaten by horses. The honey is of good quality.
Deer eat foliage and twigs, while other mammals and birds eat the
seeds, bark and leaves. Gum sometimes found on bark is soaked
in water and the liquid used as an eyewash.

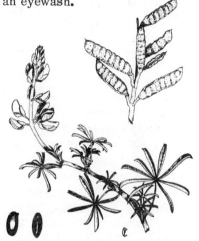

S-17. LUPINES, Lu-
pinus sp. There are a
few species of bush lu-
pines, including Lindley's
Varied Lupine, L. varii-
color (pictured).

Most
Hab.

Most
Sts.
W.
Can.

The various uses of
lupines are described on
page 42 under H-20.

S-18. EMORY'S INDI-
GO BUSH, Dalea emoryi.
Shrub densely and dif-
fusely branched, 1-4' high;
leaves in clusters of 5-7 leaflets; small branchlets spiny; pea-
like, lavender flowers in short spikes.

Indians crushed the flowers of the
various species of Dalea and steeped
them in water to release a yellow dye
used in art work. A dye was also extracted from the glandular twigs. The
roots of Dalea terminalis have a sweet
taste and were eaten like candy by the
Hopi. Flowers were also used medicinally and for food.

Des.

Cal.
Ar.
Nev.

A tea made by boiling the stems was
used as a remedy for many ailments
including: colds, coughs, pneumonia,
tuberculosis, stomach ache, snall pox,
kidney trouble, veneral disease, measles, muscle pains, and diarrhea.

Stems were chewed for toothache;
crushed stems used for sores.

S-19. CREOSOTE BUSH, <u>Larrea divaricata</u>; Caltrops Fam. An erect-growing and many branched bush from 2'-9' tall; leaves appear divergently 2-lobed; yellow flowers solitary and terminal; foliage very resinous and strong-smelling. The roots put out an inhibitor to keep other plants from growing too near. But, in seasons of heavy or frequent rains the inhibitor is washed from the ground and then you will see flowers and small plants growing around these bushes. As the soil dries,   the inhibitor starts again and the neighbors leave in a short time.

Des.

Cal.
Nev.
Ut.
Ar.
N. M.
Tex.

Creosote yields a coloring matter, and a gum (lac) secreted by a scale insect, which the Indians used to attach arrow tips to the shafts of fire-hardened wood.

Creosote was considered to be a cure-all by many Indians. A decoction of the leaves was used for stomach disorders, chicken pox, kidney trouble, colds, snake bites, rheumatism, venereal diseases, sores, and tetanus. Powdered dry leaves used for sores.   Strong tea used for tonic and mixed with badger oil as a burn ointment. The Spaniards used a preparation for sick cattle and saddle gall on horses.

S-20. GOAT NUT or JOJOBA, <u>Simmondsia</u> <u>chinensis</u>; Box Fam.   3'-10' high bush, with gray-green leaves; the rather nondescript-colored,   greenish flowers form head-like clusters,   each turning into a smooth, brown, cylindrical capsule like an acorn. Forms a very good   stock feed on heavily grazed land.

Des.
Chap.

Cal.
Ar.

Indians used seeds by roasting and grinding them for a beverage; oil of the seed was used as a hair tonic. Fruit has a nutty flavor and   early Californians made a beverage that was used as a coffee substitute, by roasting and grinding nuts,   mixing them with yolks of hard-boiled eggs, then boiling with milk and sugar.

S-21. SCARLET SU-MAC, Rhus glabra; Sumac Fam. A large shrub or small tree, with fern-like leaves, greenish flowers and bunches of red fruit which contain malic acid. The dried ripe fruit is slightly sour, astringent and diuretic (increasing a flow of urine).

SW

Most Sts. W. Can.

Indians crushed the fruit to make a drink and also dried berries for winter use. The split bark and stems were used in basket making. They gathered leaves after turning red for smoking and roots for a yellow dye. A poultice was made of bruised leaves and fruit and applied to the skin for skin diseases.

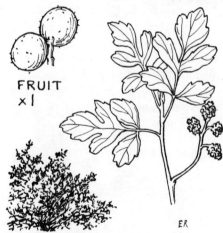

FRUIT
x I

S-22. SQUAW BUSH or SKUNK BUSH, Rhus trilobata. 2'-7' high bush, of rocky foothills. Pale yellow flowers appear before leaves; berries red and hairy.

Parkinson (1640) writes about genus that both Pliny and Dioscorides say: "A decoction of leaves or seed made with vinegar and a little honey is quite good against gangrene or cankers. Juice taken out of leaves by boiling them in water and, after they are strained, boil them again with some honey. Helps the roughness of tongue and throat. Decoction of green leaves makes the hair black. Plant is much used in wardrobes, chests, etc. to keep out moths -."

Chap. Oak

Most Sts.

Brooks Botany says its astringent properties made it useful in tanning leather. Indians powdered berries, making a lotion used in treatment of small-pox. Dry powder was put on open sores, but when pustules were unopen, the lotion was put on. The fruit is

eaten and a stem decoction is good for coughs. Peeled and split stems used for twined baskets. Lemonade Berry, <u>Rhus integrifolia</u>, has red berries used in making drink. Sugar Sumac, <u>Rhus ovata</u>,

(Rhus integrifolia)

(R. ovata)

has a sweetish, waxen substance covering the red berries, which was used by the Indians to make sugar.

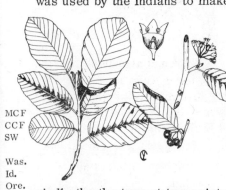

MCF
CCF
SW

Was.
Id.
Ore.
Mont.
Cal.
W.
Can.

S-23. CASCARA SAGRADA, <u>Rhamnus Purshiana</u>; Buckthorn Fam. An attractive shrub, 4'-6' high in south; up to 30' in the north, where it is fine bee plant.

Early Spanish settlers learned from the Indians of its wonderful medicincal qualities, and called it Cascara Sagrada, or "sacred bark." Indians would girdle the the tree at two points three feet apart and make vertical cuts between, then peel off the bark and dry it for medicinal use as a cathartic. For best results bark should be gathered in autumn or early spring before using. A small piece of bark put in cold water for 12 hours is used for a tonic.

Most
Hab.

Most
Sts.
W.
Can.

S-24. CEANOTHUS (also called Wild Lilac, Sweet Bush, Buck Brush, Deer Brush, Blue Blossom), <u>Ceanothus</u> sp. (The species shown is Common Buck Brush, <u>C. cuneatus</u>). 2-20' high bush or small tree, with rigid, sometimes spine-like, branchlets; leaves with tiny stipules at the base; blossoms white through

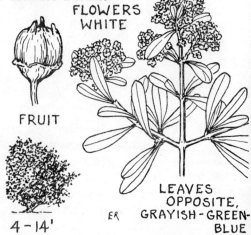

FLOWERS
WHITE

FRUIT

4 - 14'

LEAVES
OPPOSITE,
GRAYISH-GREEN-
BLUE

blue or lavender, borne on plumy spikes and usually giving off a spicy odor; commonest on open slopes where there is good drainage. It gives fine protection from erosion and is good in gardens.

The Indians used the seed as food and the blossoms as a fine lather when rubbed briskly on the skin. The leaves are suitable for use as a tobacco; bark and roots are used as an astringent and tonic. The red roots also yield a red dye.

The plant has medicinal properties serviceable today. One variety is beneficial as a blood coagulant, also for coughing and tonsilitis, and as a stimulant tonic for mucous membranes. It overcomes mal-assimilation of food, and influences beneficially acute inflammation of the liver and spleen.

S-25. CALIFORNIA FREMON-TIA, Fremontia californica; Sterculia Fam. Also called Flannel Bush. A scraggly-growing shrub 6-15' high on slopes from 1500 to 5500' altitude. Leaves have a brown soft fuzz underneath; flowers are a lovely yellow, borne all along the branches, making an extremely beautiful sight in early spring; the 4-5 celled capsule has grayish-brown seeds. Local people call it "Slippery Elm", as the inner bark is quite mucilaginous when wet.

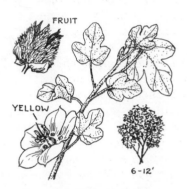

PJ
MCF
CCF
Chap.

Cal.

The inner bark is used as a demulcent for poultices (a soothing agent for raw membranes). Cattle will browse the twigs, which are very nutritious.

S-26. BEARBERRY, Arctostaphylos uva-ursi; Heath Fam. A low growshrub, found in large mats, usually between 3000' to 9000' altitudes; white, urn-shaped flowers; red berries.

Most Hab.

Indians used the leaves in their smoking tobacco and called it Kinnikinnick. Dry leaves in the fall are astringent, and picked for a tonic, also as a

Most Sts.

cleaning lotion. Plant boiled is used for tea and and for ordinary stomach trouble. Foliage contains tannin. Pioneers made a decoction of the leaves for poison oak.

S-27.   MANZANITA, Arctostaphylos sp.   The two most common species are the Green Leaf (A. patula, illustrated), and the Grey Leaf (A. mewukka) or Indian Manzanita. Both of these will not fire-kill, but send out new shoots from the large, round root crowns.   A few other species do. All are evergreen shrubs with very crooked branches; the attractive,

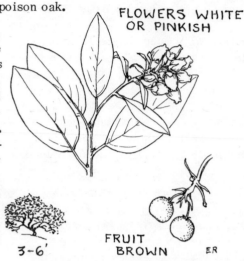

FLOWERS WHITE OR PINKISH

3-6'

FRUIT BROWN   ER

CCF
MCF
Chap.
Oak

Was.
Ore.
Cal.
Nev.
Ut.
Ar.

small, urn-shaped, pink or white flowers in small, nodding terminal clusters. The berries are round and of many colors, but are chiefly various shades of red and pink.

Indians made many uses of the berries, eating them raw, cooked or ground into meal to be used as a porridge. They ranked next to acorns in food value. A cider was made from the berries, which were crushed, and then scalded with enough water to equal the bulk of the berries. When settled, this made a fine drink. A jelly is also made from the Grey Leaf Manzanita and some other species.

In a medicinal way, fruits and leaves were crushed for their astringent properties for relief of bronchitis, dropsy and other diseases. A tea made of the berries was used as a wash for poison oak.   The leaves were crushed and dried and mixed with tobacco to make up a smoke.

The shrub is a decorative one for gardens and has the advantage of growing on stony soil of poor fertility. Crooked branches of many of these shrubs are used in dry decorations, some being sunblasted to given them a light tan driftwood appearance; others are left with the natural red color. The leaves in both cases are removed.

Manzanita is poor forage for cattle, but many animals eat it.

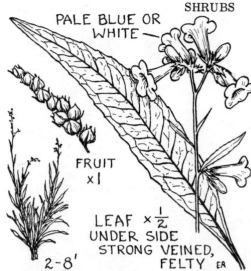

PALE BLUE OR WHITE —

FRUIT x1

LEAF x$\frac{1}{2}$
UNDER SIDE
STRONG VEINED,
2-8'   FELTY ER

S-28. YERBA SANTA, Eriodictyon californicum; Phacelia Fam. 2-8' tall shrub, with leaves distinctively woolly on the undersides and with strongly netted veins, the upper surface shining; flowers of terminal panicles shade from dark lavender through pale lavender to white.

Chap.
Oak
SW
CCF
MCF
Ore.
Cal.

Indians boiled leaves for tea and used for colds; they mashed leaves as a poultice for abrasions and also to keep down swelling and to help pain. Leaves and flowers were steeped in hot water to alleviate coughs, stomach-aches, vomiting, diarrhea, venereal diseases and rheumatism. The plant is valuable also for a fine grade of amber honey with a slightly spicy flavor.

S-29. BLUE CURLS, VINEGAR-WEED or CAMPHOR WEED, Trichostema sp.; Mint Fam. Woolly Blue Curls, T. lanatum (pictured) is a shrub, but most other species of this genus are herbs. The shrub is 2'-4' tall, but the herbs range from 3"-16". The

Most
Hab.

Was.
Ore.
Cal.
Id.

shrub has blue or purple flowers (rarely white) and more or less hairy leaves. The name of Vinegar Weed comes from the penetrating and acrid odor of the foliage of all species.

FLOWERS
PURPLE
WOOLLY

x$\frac{1}{2}$

Indians made a decoction of leaves and flowers for colds, ague and general debility; a bath of this decoction was taken against small pox; leaves were chewed and put in cavity of aching tooth; fresh leaves were mashed and thrown in streams to stupify fish. A major honey plant.

ER

S-30. MONKEY FLOWER, <u>Mimulus</u> sp.; Figwort Fam. This genus has a few shrubs, including the Orange Bush Monkey Flower, <u>M</u>. <u>aurantiacus</u> (shown in picture). Uses of monkey flowers are described on page 55 under H-47.

Most Hab.
Most Sts.
W.
Can.

LEAVES DEEP GREEN

FLOWERS ORANGE

2-5'

× ½

ER

S-31. PENSTEMON, <u>Penstemon</u> sp. Most of these are herbs and their uses are described on page 56 under H-49.

Most Hab.
Most Sts.
W.
Can.

S-32. BLUEBERRY ELDER, <u>Sambucus</u> <u>caerulea</u>, and <u>S</u>. <u>mexicana</u>; Honeysuckle Fam. These species are very closely alike, but <u>mexicana</u> usually has 3-5 leaflets in a compound leaf, while <u>caerulea</u> has 5-9 leaflets. Both species are bushes or small trees, 6-15' high, with small white, flowers in terminal clusters turning into bluish berries.

Most Hab.

Most Sts.
W.
Can.

The Indians call it "the tree of music", as they make flutes from branches that were cut in the spring and then dried with the leaves on. When thoroughly dry, they would bore holes in the branches with a hot stick. The large shoots were used for arrow shafts. Berries were used in several ways, for a drink and also dried and stored for winter. Flowers were used fresh externally in a decoction for an antiseptic wash for skin diseases and taken internally to check bleeding of the lungs. The inner bark yields a strong emetic.

Fine wine is made from the berries. When the berries are ripe, they are gathered and dried in the sun, then put away for winter pies. Dried berries are boiled in sugar when making pies. Small flowers are beaten in batter for pancakes or muffins. The flowers heads are dipped in a batter and quickly fried, making a delicious fritter.

Song birds, bandtailed pigeons and grouse are fond of the berries. Among the animals; rabbits, squirrels, chipmunks, mice, and rats eat the fruit and bark; deer eat the foliage. The white wood is used for skewers and pegs. A decoction of the leaves is supposed to keep caterpillars from eating plants.

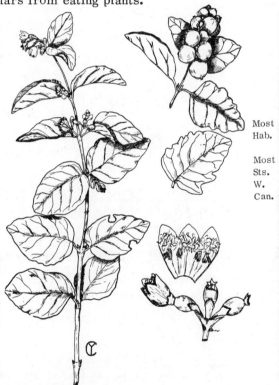

S-33. SNOWBERRY, WAXBERRY, or INDIAN CURRANT, Symphoricarpos sp. Erect shrubs of low or medium height, with slender branches, sometimes prostrate and sometimes spreading by suckers; leaves opposite, round or oval; white or rosy flowers appear in terminal or axillary clusters; round, waxy-white berries.

Saponin, a poisonous drug, is contained in the leaves only. Indians made a decoction for colds and stomach-ache by pounding and steeping the roots. The fruits act as an emetic and cathartic (strong laxative). As a honey plant, it is fairly important, producing a white honey.

Most Hab.

Most Sts. W. Can.

Snowberries are highly regarded as ornamental shrubs due to the striking-looking bunches of fruit and lovely leaves. It is an important wild-life food, as the berries remain on the bushes most of the year. Birds use the bushes as protective shelter.

HERBS

The colors of flowers, fruits, seeds, etc. that are given on this page should be used in the field to help you with quick identification of the species you encounter, but should not be used alone. Carefully study the descriptions and pictures of all species before making up your mind that you have made correct identifications.

FLOWER COLORS

Blue or bluish: 5, 20, 41, 42, 43, 49, 50.

Brown or brownish: 10, 49.

Green or greenish: 1, 3, 4, 8, 10, 11, 12, 24, 40, 46.

Purple, violet or lavender: 6, 20, 21, 22, 25, 28, 29, 30, 31, 37, 40, 41, 42, 43, 47, 49, 56, 58.

Red, rose or pink: 2, 6, 9, 13, 14, 15, 16, 20, 21, 25, 27, 28, 31, 34, 38, 39, 40, 47, 49, 50, 58, 60.

White or whitish: 2, 3, 4, 5, 6, 7, 9, 12, 13, 14, 16, 18, 19, 20, 21, 22, 28, 29, 31, 32, 33, 34, 37, 37, 39, 41, 44, 45, 46, 48, 49, 50, 57, 58, 59, 60.

Yellow or yellowish or orange: 6, 15, 16, 17, 20, 21, 22, 26, 35, 37, 40, 46, 47, 48, 49, 50, 51, 52, 53, 54, 55, 56, 57, 58, 59.

FRUIT AND SEED COLORS
(Not all fruits and seeds are listed here.)

B = berries; C = capsules; F = fruits; N = nutlets; P = pods; S = seeds; Sp. = spores.

Black: 2 (S), 3 (S) 11 (B), 12 (S), 13 (S), 15 (S), 19 (S), 45 (B), 53 (S), 59 (S).

Brown or reddish-brown: 9 (F), 10 (F), 18 (S), 20 (P), 21 (P), 22 (P), 23 (S), 29 (S), 30 (S), 31 (S), 32 (S), 39 (S), 40 (S), 41 (S), 42 (S), 43 ( ), 43 (S), 46 (S), 47 (S), 48 (S), 49 (S), 50 (C).

Gray or grayish: 14 (S), 24 (S), 30 (S), 31 (S), 36 (S), 52 (S), 53 (S)

Green or greenish: 1 (SP), 4 (S), 6 (C), 7 (F), 21 (P), 22 (P).

Purplish or red: 12 (B), 37 (F).

Whitish-brown: 41 (S), 42 (S).   Yellow or yellowish: 17 (S).

H-1. HORSETAIL, <u>Equisetum</u> sp. See page 3 under W-2.

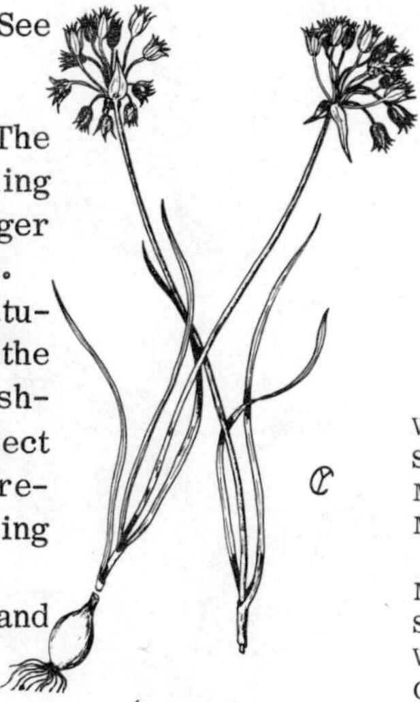

H-2. WILD ONIONS, <u>Allium</u> sp. The long, slender leaves and the onion-smelling foliage are typical. It was mainly the larger species with large bulbs that Indians used.

Aztecs chewed the bulbs to relieve flatulency and as food. California Indians ate the bulbs raw and cooked them also over hot ashes. The whole plant was used as an insect repellant by rubbing on the body. It is reputed to be useful as a diuretic (increasing the flow of urine) in kidney disorders.

Flowers are rose, reddish-purple and white in color; leaves 2-4" or more high.

Wtr.
SW
Md.
Msh

Most
Sts.
W.
Can.

H-3. INDIAN SOAP ROOT, or AMOLE, <u>Chlorogalum</u>. 2'-3' tall herb, with narrow, fluted leaves, a brown, fibrously coated bulb, and large white flowers with green veins.

Indians dug up the large bulb and stripped off the outer fibrous mesh, which was left to dry. These dried fibers became a fine brush, being tightly tied together with more fibers at one end for the handle. The inner mucilaginous layer was scraped and worked into the handle, then put in the sun for a day or two to harden.

Most
Hab.

Most
Sts.
W.
Can.

Gr.

Oak

Cal.

The bulb was also boiled, which took out the soapy material, and was then eaten as are potatoes. Or the bulb was baked in an earthen oven, and eaten or dried and stored over the winter; in that case, it must be boiled before eating. It was also used as a soap for washing hair or clothes. Mashed and scattered in streams, it stupified fish, which could then be easily netted.

The bulb was also used as an antiseptic for sores and ulcers, and as a diuretic and laxative. When the bulb was roasted, the exuding juice was used as glue for arrow feathers.

H-4. FALSE HELLEBORE, Veratrum californicum; Bunch Flower Fam. (see illustration above). 3-7' tall plant (sometimes called Skunk Cabbage), with large, heavily-ribbed leaves which gradually grow smaller as they reach the top of the plant. Flowers are a dull greenish-white, borne on a showy, elongated terminal cluster. Roots are few and extremely black.

Msh
Md.
MCF
CCF

The plant inhabits moist meadows and along streams at middle altitudes in mountains. Blossoms are said to be poisonous to many insects. Powdered roots are used as an insecticide. The dry root, powdered, was used as a snuff.

Most
Sts.
W.
Can.

Parkinson writes in 1640: "Roots were most used. Half a dram of oxymel (honey and vinegar), or juice of the quince, or a quince put in the roots was baked in an oven or roasted under embers. A scruple of juice given after eating was used for sufferers of melancholy, dizziness, breaking out on the skin, and mixed with lye and applied to the skin for removal of tics." Being a dangerous medicine, it must be taken with caution. He adds: "The Spaniards made a poison from the juice of the roots, which, after fermenting, was used on arrow heads. The antidote was eating quinces. Animals killed with the poison were considered good eating, as the flesh was more tender and pleasant."

The Shoshones and other Indians used the raw root, crushed and mashed, to apply to snake bite wounds on man and animals. A decoction of the root was taken as a tea for venereal disease. The raw root, chewed, aided sore throats, inflamed tonsils and colds.

H-5. COMMON CAMASS, <u>Camassia quamash</u>; Lily Fam. 5 species occur in the west. About 2' tall, with single, tall flower stalk coming from middle; flowers mostly a brilliant blue, but sometimes almost white. Grows in moist ground and wet meadows.

Bulbs are very nutritious and are highly thought of by Indians who will travel a long way to gather them. After the seeds are ripe in the spring, they dig up the bulbs with long, crooked sticks (usually made of Mt. Mahogany). Then a fairly deep hole is made and lined with fire-heated stones. Bulbs are placed inside and covered with hot ashes and stones and allowed to cook for 24 hours. They are eaten right from the fire or the black outer coating is peeled off and the bulb pressed by hand into a flat cake and hung to dry in sacks, becoming a tid-bit at feasts.

A molasses was also made of bulbs by boiling in water until it was almost evaporated. The early California settlers learned the value of the bulbs and would make pies of them. But eaten to excess, the bulb will act as a purgative and emetic. The greenish-white flowers of the Death Camass often grow with the blue and care must be used in digging bulbs.

Md.
MCF
CCF

Most
Sts.

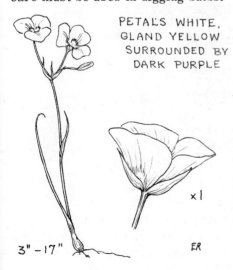

PETALS WHITE,
GLAND YELLOW
SURROUNDED BY
DARK PURPLE

×1

3" – 17"

ER

H-6. SEGO LILY, <u>Calochortus nuttallii</u>. There were several species of Calochortus Lily used by the Indians. All are told by the few, showy flowers (white, rose, purple, red or yellow), each with petals marked with dark spots, blotches or lines.

Indians dug the bulbs when first flower buds appeared, roasted them in ashes after fire had died down, and also steamed them. Seeds were parched for pinole meal.

Gr.
Oak
MCF
Sage
PJ

Most
Sts.

MCF
Md.
SW

Cal.
Ar.
Nev.
N. M.
Tex.

H-7. YERBA MANSA, <u>Anemopsis</u> <u>californica</u>; Lizard's Tail Fam. 6-24" tall plant, with a creeping root-stock, white flowers in dense spikes surrounded by petal-like bracts; the heart-shaped leaves are mostly basal. The plant has a pungent, spicy odor, and the aromatic root was chewed raw.

Tea made of the leaves was used for purifying blood; a poultice for cuts and bruises; and bruised leaves reduced swellings, dysentery, ashma. The tea was also used for colds and to help movement of urine in kidney ailments. An infusion of the root-stocks was used for various skin troubles. The leaves boiled in a quantity of water were used as a bath for muscular pains and for sore feet. Dried roots, roasted and browned, were made into a decoction used for colds and for stomach ache.

CCF
MCF
Md.
SW

Most
Sts.

H-8. NETTLES, <u>Urtica</u> species. The 6 western species are all covered with stinging hairs, and have opposite, 3-7 nerved; toothed leaves; the flowers form cluster at the axils of the hairy or smooth leaves.

Pepys, in 1661, speaks of eating nettle porridge; also eaten in northern Persia. Scotch and Irish use the young leaves for greens. The French make 7 different dishes from the nettle tops. Stems have an excellent fibre, used for fish lines and clothes.

FLOWERS
×1

×½

1~10'

FRUIT

ER

Indians used branches to strike parts affected by pains, and a decoction of roots to bathe rheumatic pains in joints. Sometimes, pounded leaves rubbed on limbs produced a counter-irritant. Hot poultices of the mashed leaves were used for rheumatism.

H-9.   WILD BUCK-
WHEAT, Eriogonum sp.
Buckwheat Family (E.
baileyi illustrated right).
There are about 150 spe-
cies in a growth range
from sea level to high
mountains. All varieties
seem to like more or less
dry and rocky slopes and
ridges. Most buckwheats
grow on medium   tall
stems, loosely branched,
with white to pinkish flowers in clusters or heads.

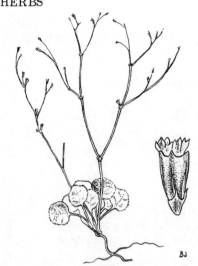

Because of its long blooming season and fine quality honey,
buckwheat is an excellent bee plant, but it is poor stock feed.

From the leaves Indians made a decoction for headache and
stomach pains; also a tea from the flowers was used as an eye-
wash and for high blood pressure and bronchial ailments.   The
stems and leaves are boiled for a tea to treat bladder trouble.

H-10.   CURLY DOCK, Rumex crispus. 1'-4' high herb with
dark green foliage; the leaves have very wavy margins and are
crisp. It is a naturalized weed from Europe.

Ancient Arabs used the roots for purging and some took a decoction with beer or ale to
purge the liver and cleanse
the blood.   A decoction of
roots in vinegar was a most
effective remedy for scales
and running sores. Dios-
corides said the root eaten
took away the pain of stings
by scorpions.

Leaves are used often as
pot herbs and as an antidote
to scurvy; also as a mild astringent and, in small doses,
as a tonic. Indians cut roots
and steeped in boiling water

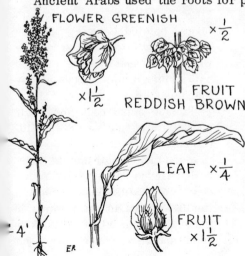

FLOWER GREENISH

$\times \frac{1}{2}$

$\times 1\frac{1}{2}$

FRUIT
REDDISH BROWN

LEAF $\times \frac{1}{4}$

FRUIT
$\times 1\frac{1}{2}$

for a tonic and a stomach remedy; also, they washed roots and applied them to sores and swellings.

FLOWERS GREENISH ×6

H-11. LAMB'S QUARTERS, GOOSEFOOT or SOWBANE, Chenopodium sp.; Goosefoot Fam. (C. murale, Nettle - leaved Goosefoot, illustrated.) Usually many - branched plants, 1'-4' tall, with small green flowers on spiked panicles; often strongly scented. Many species are introduced weeds.

Most Hab.

Most Sts. W. Can.

8-15"   ×½   FR

Indians boiled the leaves as spinach, sometimes eating them raw. They would gather the seeds and grind them into a meal to be stored for future uses, such as bread making. One variety was boiled and applied as a poultice to reduce swellings: also, used in the mouth to relieve toothache. For rheumatism, the affected parts were washed with a decoction of the leaves.

Clt.

Cal.

H-12. POKEWEED, PIGEON BERRY, RED INK PLANT, Phytolacca sp.; Pokeweed Fam. A large, coarse herb, 3-4' high, with large, pointed leaves, purplish stem, thick fleshy root; greenish-white flowers in racemes; berries with crimson juice; seeds glossy black-purple.

Indians dried root and fruit, and used as purgative and emetic. Chinese dug root of one species in second and eighth month. They boiled leaves as pot herb. Young pokeweed shoots can be dug in the spring, boiled in two waters; in second water a bit of fat pork is added and all is served as greens with vinegar. The plant contains a bitter acidic poison, saponin, the root being most poisonous. From large roots, pokeweed shoots will renew themselves again and again after each cutting (cut at a foot or 2 high, before turning purple), furnishing an excellent winter and early spring vegetable if kept away from frost. Medicinally the root was used for skin diseases, rheumatism and glandular swellings. It acts on the thyroid gland. The juice of the berries was used for coloring frosting and candies.

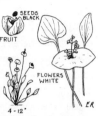

H-13. MINER'S LETTUCE, Montia perfolia-ta, Purslane Fam. A dainty-looking plant with 6"-12" high stems; and narrow, basal leaves. Halfway up the stems, disks or cups completely encircle the stem. Above this, on a continuation of the stem, are clusters of pink or white flowers.

MCF
CCF
Oak
Chap.

Most
Sts.

Fleshy, tender leaves are eaten green or cooked by the Indians, who also made a tea of the plant and used it as a laxative. The miners used the leaves as salad greens, hence the name.

H-14. BITTERROOT, Lewisia rediviva. This perennial herb is almost stemless, with a rosette of oblong fleshy leaves growing at the top of a carrot-shaped root. The large rose or white flowers have 8-15 petals. Related species have similar qualities.

Indians would gather the root in the spring when the outer coating, which contains most of the bitterness, will slip off easily when put in boiling water. The root is quite starchy, but very

Sage
Chap.
Oak
MCF
CCF

Most
Sts.
W.
Can.

nutritious and was an important food among the Indians. In fact, so much importance was given to it that a sackful of the roots was considered a good exchange for a horse. The roots were often dried for winter use, and were boiled with other wild foods in a soup. Pounded dry root was chewed for sore throat.

CCF
MCF
Chap.
Oak
SA
Alp.

H-15. COLUMBINE, Aquilegia sp.; Crowfoot Fam. (A. formosa, Northwest Crimson Columbine, illustrated on next page.) Most species grow in moist situations along streams or in meadows. They vary in height from a few inches to 5'. Flowers are

Most
Sts.
W.
Can.

red or yellow, 5-petaled, with long hollow spurs extending backward.

Parkinson writes in 1640, "Leaves commonly used in lotions for sore mouths and throats. A dram of seeds taken in wine with saffron opens obstructions of liver, and good for jaundice, causing profuse sweating." Spaniards used to eat a piece of the root in the morning on fast days. The Indians often boiled and ate the leaves in the spring. The boiled roots were used in a tea to stop diarrhea. The ripe seeds were mashed, moistened and then vigorously rubbed in the hair to discourage head lice. Fresh roots were mashed and rubbed on aching joints. When roots and leaves are boiled together it makes a decoction that can be taken in one-half cupful doses several times daily for a couple of days to stop biliousness or dizziness. If the whole plant is boiled it is supposed, as a decoction taken in small doses, to stop veneral diseases.

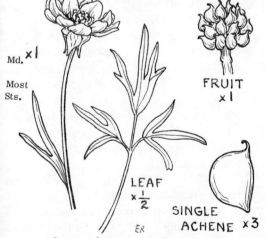

Md. x1

Most Sts.

FRUIT x1

LEAF x½

SINGLE ACHENE x3

H-16. BUTTERCUPS, Ranunculus sp. (R. Californicus, California Buttercup, illustrated). Usually showy yellow (sometimes white or red) flowers, 8"-24" high, rising from more or less basal leaves.

Young flowers are preserved in vinegar as small pickles. The juice of flowers makes a yellow dye. Indians parched seeds and made meal to use in bread. Roots were boiled and eaten. One

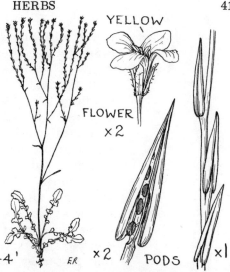

YELLOW

FLOWER
x2

-4'   ER   x2   PODS   x1

Des.
Gr.
Oak
Sage
Chap.

species, <u>Ranunculus scel-
eratus</u>; Cursed Buttercup,
has a poison, aenonal, that
causes intestinal inflamation. If the acrid, burning
juice is tasted, spit it out.

H-17. HEDGE MUS-
TARD, <u>Descurainia pin-
natum</u>; Mustard Fam. Also called Western Tansy
Mustard. 2' tall, erect
plant; leaves once or twice
divided into small seg-
ments, ashy color. Small,
yellow flowers appear on long slender stems. Found in dry areas.

Most
Sts.

The Mexican name is Pamito and is sold in their drug stores.
The seeds are crushed and used as poultices or made into a tea
for summer complaint. Leaves, picked young, are good boiled.

Indians gathered seeds by knocking them into baskets. The
seeds were stirred over an open fire in a pan, then ground and
made into a mush or stirred into soup. Pomo Indians mixed the
seeds with their corn meal for better taste. In Mexico the seeds
were made into a poultice for wounds. Brooks wrote: "It is said
to be an attenuate, expectorant and diuretic, and is strongly recommended in chronic coughs and hoarseness."

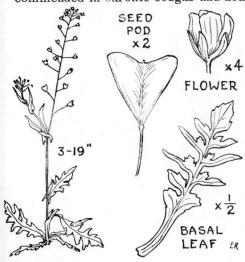

SEED
POD
x2

x4
FLOWER

3-19"

x½

BASAL
LEAF ER

H-18. SHEPHERD'S
PURSE, <u>Capsella bursa-
pastoris</u>. 3"-24" tall
herb; stem single, with
branching, deeply cut basal leaves that have a pep-
pery flavor; tiny white flowers become triangular pods.

Most
Hab.

Most
Sts.
W.
Can.

Used as a pot herb, it
tastes like cabbage; also
young leaves eaten raw.
Indians roasted seeds and
used as a nutritious meal.

An infusion of 1 ounce of

MCF
CCF
SW

Ore.
Was.
Cal.
Id.
W.
Can.

leaves in 12 quarts of water is a remedy for bruises; taken internally it stops bleeding.

H-19.   ALUM ROOT, <u>Heuchera</u> <u>micrantha</u>, Saxifrage Fam.   1'-2 1/2' tall perennial, with stout rootstock (having alum-like taste); basal leaves round and toothed; long flowering stems have panicles of small white flowers.

Indians eat leaves first in the Spring, boiled and steamed. After steaming, some are dried and stored for future use.   The pounded root, wet, was used on sores and swellings; steeped, it was used as an eye-wash; also small amounts drunk to stop diarrhea.   A tonic of the boiled roots was taken a half-cupful a day for general debility, or three half cups a day to stop fever. The drug, Heuchera, is antiseptic and astringent.   In <u>Materia</u> <u>Medica,</u> alumroot is given for gastorenteritis, nausea, vomiting, etc.

H-20. LUPINES, <u>Lupinus</u> sp., Pea Fam. (<u>L.</u> <u>andersonii</u>, Anderson's Lupine, in illustration).   Mainly perennial herbs with palmately-compound leaves; pea-like flowers on long stalks, mostly blue, but some flowers are yellow, white, purplish or reddish-colored.   A widespread genus, good forage, and ploughed-under is a good fertilizer.

Virgil called it "Sad Lupine", as seeds were used by the poor, being boiled to remove bitter taste.   In 1640,   Parkinson   wrote: "seed meal and honey takes away black and blue spots. "

Most
Hab.

Indians made a tea from the seeds and used it medicinally, especially to help urination.   Early in the Spring, leaves and flowers were   stripped off   and steamed, then eaten with acorn soup. Seeds often dangerous because of alkaloids.

Most
Sts.
W.
Can.

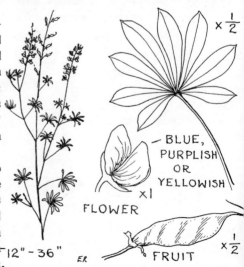

x 1/2

— BLUE, PURPLISH OR YELLOWISH

x1

FLOWER

12" - 36"

ER

FRUIT   x 1/2

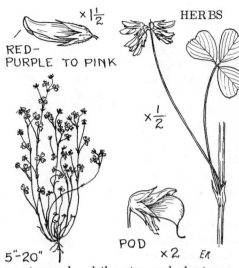

×1½

RED-
PURPLE TO PINK

×½

5"-20"

POD ×2 EA

H-21. WILD CLOVER,
Trifolium sp. (*T.* graci-
lentum, Pinpoint Clover,
illustrated). Small herbs
with typical 3 leaflets and
flowers yellow, white or
purple in heads or short
spikes; stamen 2-grouped.

In Scotland, bread was
made from the White Clov-
er (*T. repens*), and the
pioneers made clover tea,
brewing dried flower
heads. Indians ate it raw

Most
Hab.

Most
Sts.
W.
Can.

or steamed and the steamed plant was dried for winter use.

White clover was not cooked, but eaten raw, both flowers and
leaves, but if too much was consumed, it would produce bloat, and,
to counteract this effect, the leaves were dipped in salted water.

H-22. LOCO WEED, *Astragalus* sp. (*A.* bicristatus, Crested
Rattle-weed, illustrated). Usually bushy herbs with long stalks;
leaves with several to many leaflets, alternate; flowers in spikes,
racemes or heads, purple, pale yellow or white.

Most
Hab.

Most
Sts.

Indians chewed the plant to
cure sore throats and to reduce
swellings. The boiled root was
made into a decoction to wash
granulated eyelids and for tooth-
aches.

The plant seems to be more
toxic in some soils than in others.
It is poisonous to practically all
stock, although, after they have
once tasted it, it is much sought
after by them. It is said that if
poisoned stock are fed hot lard
and moved immediately to new
pasture, they may survive.

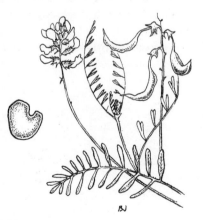

Gr.
Md.
Oak
MCF

Most
Sts.
W.
Can.

H-23. PRAIRIE FLAX, <u>Linum lewisii</u>, Flax Fam. 8-36" high herb, many-branched, erect-growing and with woody root stock; flowers blue in terminal clusters.

57.

Indians used seeds in cookings, as they have a pleasant taste and are highly nutritious. Stems steeped for stomach disorders, and roots were steeped for eye medicine. Fiber was used as string. The whole plant was mashed and soaked in cold water to make an eye medicine. Poultices of the crushed fresh leaves were used to reduce swellings, especially goiter and for gall trouble. Early settlers made a poultice of the powdered seed, corn meal and boiling water, mixing this into a paste for infected wounds and mumps.

<u>Pharmacopia</u> says, "Reported useful in rehumatism, catarrhal infections, liver complaints and dropsy."

Sage
Gr.
Oak
Clt.

Was.
Ore.
Cal.

H-24. TURKEY MULLEIN, <u>Eremocarpus setigerus</u>, Spurge Fam. A low-growing bush, 5-8" high, with heavy-scented gray foliage, in dry, open areas from Washington to Lower California. Greenish flowers; dark gray, shining seeds; stinging hairs.

As the leaves contain a narcotic poison, Indians used the foliage to stupify fish and poison their arrow points. A poultice relieved internal chest pains and a decoction of leaves in warm water helped asthma and fevers. <u>Pharmacopia</u> says used to expel gas.

H-25. HIGH MALLOW, <u>Malva</u> <u>sylvestrus</u>, Mallow Fam. Erect or branching herb, 1-3 1/2' high, with rounded, heart-shaped leaves; small flowers are pink-veined against purple, appearing clustered or single. Grows in waste places and in cultivated fields.

Clt.
Gr.
Sage

Pliny wrote, "that anyone taking a spoonful of mallows will be free of disease; they soften and heal ulcers and sores." Parkinson wrote: "Leaves and roots boiled in wine or water or in both with parsley doth help to open the body, for hot agues. Leaves bruised and laid on the eyes with a little honey take away the inflammation from them."

Most
Sts.
W.
Can.

Chinese eat the leaves raw in salad or boiled as spinach. Spanish-Americans use the plants by boiling leaves and making a wash for any bodily disease; headaches are cured by adding salt and vinegar to mashed leaves. Indians use leaves, soft stems and flowers, steeped and made into a poultice for running sores, boils and swellings. An infusion of dried leaves is good for coughs.

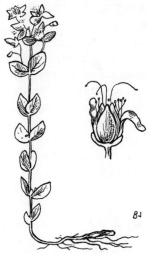

H-26. St. JOHN'S WORT or KLAMATH WEED, <u>Hypericum</u> sp., St. John's Wort Fam. 8"-32" high plant, sending out numerous stems from a woody rootstock; opposite leaves; flowers are yellow, 5-petaled and in rather close clusters. It prefers poor, dry soil.

SW
Md.
Clt.

Parkinson (1640) wrote: "Was prepared as an ointment for external use, also as a decoction in wine to drink. A powder was made of the seeds and drunk in juice of knot grass to help all manner of spitting or vomiting of blood be it in any vein, broken inward by bruises or falls."

Most
Sts.
W.
Can.

Indians ate the fresh leaves or dried the plant and made a flour that was used in the same way as acorn meal. It was also boiled and used for running sores. A yellow dye is made by boiling in alum water. <u>H</u>. <u>scouleri</u>, Scouler's St. John's Wort (illustrated) was boiled and water used for sores, etc.

H-27. FUCHSIA, <u>Zauschneria californica</u>, Evening Primrose Fam. 1'-3' high, much branched herb, with rather fragile, green to gray-hairy leaves, and large fuchsia-like flowers. Found on dry benches and rocky hillsides.

Gr.
Oak
Sage

Cal.

Leaves reported used as a detergent in washing, and a dusting powder for cuts, wounds and sores on horses. Indians drank a decoction of leaves for tuberculosis, kidney and bladder trouble, and for a cathartic; also made into a poultice for running sores.

H-28. FIREWEED, <u>Epilobium angustifolium</u>. 1 1/2'-8' tall herb; willow-shaped, reddish leaves; lilac-purple, rose and even white flowers in long, terminal racemes.

Clt.
Md.
SW
MCF

Most
Sts.

In Europe and Asia, young shoots were used like asparagus. Canadians use young leaves and stems as a pot herb. It is used as a tea adulterate in England. Plant is astringent, and used in domestic remedies for an intestinal astringent.

It is an important range feed and honey plant.

SW
Md.
CCF
MCF
Gr.
Oak

Epilobium angustifolium

H-29. BOISDUVALIA, <u>Boisduvalia</u> sp. Usually 1'-5' tall herbs, with leafy stems; flowers small, white or purple, in axles of leaves or in leafy spikes; 4 petals, each 2-lobed. In low, damp ground.

Was.
Id.
Ore.
Cal.
Nev.
W.
Can.

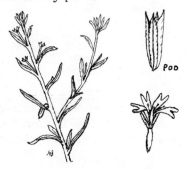

Seeds yield an oil and were also used by Indians as food. Shaken into basket and parched

Was.
Ore.
Cal.

and pulverized, they were eaten dry. Some were stored for winter use, although not parched.

H-30. CLARKIA, _Clarkia_ sp. (_C. elegans_, Elegant Clarkia, illustrated on left; _C. pulchella_, Beautiful Clarkia, on right). 1'-3' high herbs with lance-like or ovate leaves; showy, purple or rose-colored flowers in terminal, nodding racemes; petals greatly constricted at base.

Gr.
Oak
Chap.
Sage

Most
Sts.
W.
Can.

Indians collected seeds, which they dried, parched and pulverized; then ate the meal dry or with acorn meal.

H-31. LOBED GODETIA, _Godetia biloba_. 8"-30" tall herb, with narrow, alternate leaves; flowers showy, red, purple or cream colored, in racemes or spikes; petals often with purple dots near base.

Indians gathered seed pods early in the spring and hung them up in bundles to dry. When thoroughly dry, the seeds were beaten to loosen their shells, then winnowed, parched, pulverized, and stored for eating during the winter. The Indians also made a decoction for an eye wash.

Oak
Gr.

Ore.
Cal.

FLOWERS WHITE

x¼

x½

4-10'

ER

H-32. POISON HEMLOCK, _Conium maculatum_, Carrot Fam. 1 1/2'-10' tall herb, many-branched, with umbels of numerous, small, white flowers, and parsley-like leaves; grows in moist soil.

POISONOUS. Indians crushed seeds and mixed

SW
Md.
Clt.

Most
Sts.
W.
Can.

them with decomposed deer liver and used this to poison war arrows.   Young spring leaves are poisonous to cattle.   <u>Materia Medica</u> says, "used for depressed mind, loss of strength, trembling; acts on the glandular system." Thousands of pounds of leaves and seeds are imported for the drug trade each year.

H-33. SQUAWROOT or YAMPAH, <u>Per-ideridia gairdneri</u>. Also called Caraway. A tall plant with single stem, 1'-3 1/2' tall, with single umbels of white flowers, few, un-

Md.
SW

divided leaves; fleshy roots single or in clusters; several bractlets surround flowers.

Most
Sts.
W.
Can.

Parkinson, in 1640, writes: "Seeds good for colds or indigestions. A poultice made of powdered seeds is good for the eyes and will also take away black and blue spots. The herb and seed fried and put hot into a bag eases stomach pains."

The Indians gathered roots in the spring and washed them, then trampled them to release the outer skin, then washed again and cooked as potatoes. Roots were ground and made into cakes also. Fremont liked it cooked with wild duck.

H-34. BOLANDER'S YAMPAH, <u>Perideridea bolanderi</u>. 1'-2' high herb, with small, white or pinkish flowers in thick umbels; leaves opposite, the leaflets thread-like.

Sage
Md.
SA

Indians gather roots in large quantities and eat them raw or cooked as a staple article of diet - equal to Mariposa Lily bulbs. When eaten cooked, roots were boiled until mealy, peeled, and cooked as soup; this usually being done at the end of the acorn season. If stored, they were preserved by drying and washing. Found in drier parts of west, 3000'-8000' altitudes.

Ore.
Cal.
Id.
Wy.
Ut.
Nev.

H-35. ANISE, <u>Foeniculum vulgare</u>. Also called Sweet Fennel. (Illustrated on next page.) 2'-7' high herb, with very finely-divided,

grayish-light-green leaves, all with a sweet, anise smell; tiny yellow flowers in compound, flat umbels on long stems.

Parkinson, in 1640, writes: "Oil from seed sweetens breath, helps sleep, good for head and stomach consumption. Decoction with figs and licorice for coughs; boiled in wine, will help obstructions of liver; oil taken in broth helps dizziness. Plant, either green or dry, beaten and laid on eyes, will draw out bits and likewise take away hurt from (bites of) venomous creatures. Having infused bruised seed in wine 24 hours, then pressed and distilled, the residue in bottom will be like honey and can be kept for future use."

Gr.
Clt.

Cal.

Curtin, in his Healing Herbs of the Rio Grande, says: "The cavaliers of 16th Century England believed that the seed, bound in a little bag or handkerchief and kept to the nose to smell, helps men from dreaming and starting in their sleep, and causes them to rest well." The Mission Fathers would sprinkle the floors with water in which the leaves were crushed to make the floors smell sweet. Indians used seeds for digestive troubles and gathered the young shoots to use as a pot herb. Tea from the roots were used for colds and the leaves were chewed for a physic.

H-36. COW PARSNIP, <u>Heracleum</u> <u>lanatum</u>. 3-10' high herb; stout and coarse, with large leaves (up to 12" across), divided into 3 parts, hairy underneath, sawtooth edged; white flowers in umbrella-shaped, compound umbels.

Tender leaves and flower stalks are sweet, used by Indians for green food before flowers appear. The lower part of the plant was a salt substitute. Indians

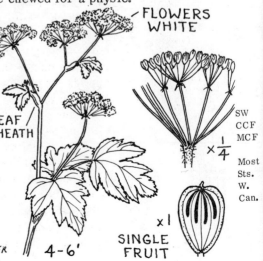

FLOWERS WHITE

LEAF / SHEATH

SW
CCF
MCF

Most
Sts.
W.
Can.

×¼

×1

SINGLE FRUIT

FR

4-6'

also cooked the roots like rutabaga. Early Spaniards made a medicine compounded from the roots for rheumatism. <u>Pharmacopia</u> says root and leaves acrid, irritant, <u>poisonous</u>; reputed carminative (useful in expelling gas); stimulant for dyspepsia (indigestion). Indians inserted root pieces in tooth cavities to stop pain. For sore throat, they mashed root, soaked in water and used infusion as a gargle, or applied it as a poultice around the throat.

H-37. CYMOPTERUS, <u>Cymopterus</u> sp. Small herbs with more or less finely-divided leaves; the yellow, white or purple flowers generally in ball-shaped umbels, often appearing perfectly round and congested; the wings or ribs of the seeds have undulate margins.

Most Hab.

Most Sts.

Basal leaves, white flowers and parsnip-like roots are eagerly sought after by Indians. They prepared them by drying and stored for later use. Only in young state can tubers be eaten. They were usually boiled. Water from old roots boiled was used as an insecticide.

H-38. SNOW PLANT, <u>Sarcodes</u> <u>sanguinea</u>, Indian Pipe Fam. The bright red stem rises from thick roots, ending in a raceme of crimson flowers. It is found in pine woods and the roots do not go down into the soil, but are covered with fungus that lives on its host and in turn supplies the plant with food from the rotting vegetation in the soil. It is thus saprophytic.

MCF CCF

Ore. Cal.

Indians dried and powdered the herb and made it into a wash for ulcers and sore mouth. It was also used to relieve toothache. The Paiutes are reported to boil the dried plant as a tea to be taken by pneumonia patients. But <u>Pharmacopia</u> says the plant is reported to be <u>poisonous.</u>

This is an example of a plant that should be used with great care on account of its possibility of poisoning the user.

H-39. COMMON DOGBANE or INDIAN HEMP, <u>Apocynum</u> <u>cannabinum</u>, Dogbane Fam. A deep-rooted plant, 1'-5' tall, with erect, smooth and pointed leaves, 2"-4" long, and terminal flowers white, pink or rose colored, in clusters. Found in shady or moist places. Most Hab.

Poisonous to stock, but usually avoided due to the bitter, rubbery juice. Indians made nets and rope from the fibers of pounded stems and roots. Seeds are eaten after being parched, and are sometimes ground into meal to make fried cakes. In New Mexico the stems of the Dogbane are broken and placed in the sun to dry and the little balls of hardened juice are used as chewing gum. The dried rhizomes and roots are used as heart stimulants and cathartics (to induce swift bowel movement). It is still in use today as a medicine for Bright's disease and irregularities of the heart. The roots are gathered in autumn.

Most Sts. W. Can.

H-40. MILKWEED, <u>Asclepias</u> sp., Milkweed Fam. (<u>A</u>. <u>mexicana</u>, Narrow-leaved Milkweed, illustrated). Usually tall, slender plants, 2-5' high; leaves 2"-6" long; flowers usually with turned-back sepals and various colors; stems show milky juice.

Poisonous to cattle and sheep, but rarely to horses. Indians dried and removed sheeth from stalk after cutting. On outside of woody center was a fibre covering. This was removed and made into string, also fish nets. Milk was collected and rolled until firm enough to make chewing gum. Green plant was collected when very small and boiled in two waters to use as greens. Pods and

GREENISH WHITE

FLOWER x 1½

x ⅓

POD WITH SEEDS

Most Hab.

Most Sts. W. Can.

stems were eaten; roots boiled and eaten with meat. Sometimes the plant was boiled and added as a thickening agent to manzanita cider. One variety was used for inflammatory rheumatism (probably <u>Asclepias</u> <u>cryptoceras,</u> which has very broad leaves with sudden, sharp points). The juice was used as healing application to cuts and wounds, also used for tattooing. Milk applied to warts, supposed to entirely cure them.

H-41. SKUNK WEED, <u>Navarre-</u> <u>tia</u> <u>squarrosa</u>; Phlox Fam.   2"-20" high herb with white woolly leaves, about 1" long, coarsely divided; flowers pale blue or purple in terminal heads; foliage has strong odor.

Gr.
Oak
MCF
CCF

Was.
Ore.
Cal.
W.
Can.

Indians gathered seeds in late summer, dried and stored them. To prepare them for eating, they would parch and pulverize the seeds and eat them dry.

Other species of <u>Navarretia</u> may have same odor and be used in same ways. White Navarretia, <u>N.</u> <u>leuco-</u> <u>cephala</u> (white flowers and with white or reddish-streaked stems), was boiled and decoction put on swellings.

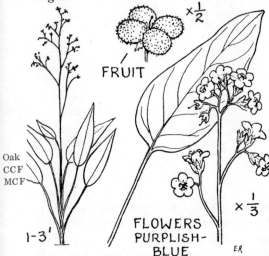

FRUIT

×½

Oak
CCF
MCF

FLOWERS
PURPLISH-
BLUE

1-3'

× ⅓

ER

H-42. GRAND HOUND'S TONGUE, <u>Cynoglossum</u> <u>grande</u>, Borage Fam. A medium-sized plant, 1-3' tall; leaves mostly basal and blue to lavender flowers are funnelform on terminal panicles. Its leaves have a disagreeable taste and the burs stick to stock.

Dioscorides says (in regard to the genus): "the leaves boiled in wine and salt applied to bruises, or juice boiled in hog lard cures falling hair; same

is good for burns.   Distilled water of herb and roots good for all purposes, inwardly to drink for ulcers and outwardly heals wounds."

Roots were cooked by the Indians and eaten to relieve colic. A poultice was made of the roots for scalds and burns.

H-43. CHIA, <u>Salvia columbaria</u>; Mint Fam. Plant grows mostly below 4000' in open, dry areas. It is 3-15" high, with 2-3 whorls of small, blue flower heads on stem.

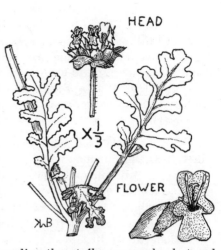

HEAD

X 1/3

FLOWER

Indians gathered seeds by bending the stalks over a basket and shaking the seeds into it. Seeds are similar to flax seed and were parched and ground to be cooked later as gruel. Medicinally, it was used to sooth inflamed digestive organs; also a bit of seed-paste put in the eye at night gathered all particles of dirt by morning due to the mucilaginous quality of the wet seed. Seed-paste is also used for soothing inflamed membranes and as a poultice for gunshot wounds. Spanish Californians made a fine drink by mixing a teaspoonful of ground seed in a glass of cold water for a few minutes, often adding sugar and lemon juice.

Sage
Chap.
Oak
Gr.
Clt.

Cal.
Ut.
Ar.
Nev.

H-44. JIMSON WEED or THORN APPLE, <u>Datura stramonium</u>, Potato Fam. 1'-5' tall plant, with stiff, spiny branches, large, coarsely-toothed leaves, white flowers trumpet-like, and sometimes tinged with light lavender; fruit prickly and about size of walnut.

Clt.
Gr.

In 1640 Parkinson wrote: "Spaniards and East Indians used this plant to dissolve gall and kidney stones." The <u>Datura</u> was used by the priests of Apollo at Delphi to produce ravings and prophecies. In India it was used by thugs and poisoners.

Dried leaves were smoked as tobacco and said to be beneficial for asthma. Mexicans and Indians called it Toloche and used it to induce a hypnotic state to unravel mysteries. In the <u>Pacific Coast Manual of Drug Plants</u> it states: "dried leaves and flowering tops - sedative, anodyne (soothing to pain), deliriant (causing delirium), depressant (lowering vital activity), and mydriatic (dilating eye)."

H-45.   SMALL-FLOWERED NIGHTSHADE, <u>Solanum</u> <u>nodiflorum.</u> Usually called Black Nightshade, because it is so much like the rarer weed, <u>S. nigrum.</u> Both have similar properties, but <u>nodiflorum</u> has 1'-2' long straggling stems, while <u>nigrum</u> is more erect, 1'-3' high, and has dull instead of shining black berries. Both have white flowers.

Clt.
Gr.
Oak
SW

Most
Sts.

Berries are POISONOUS, but boiling destroys the toxic properties in the ripe, black berries, and they are often made into pies. Although the old leaves are poisonous, it is said that young leaves and stems can be boiled as a pot herb. Indians used a decoction as an eye-wash. Parkinson wrote: "The root boiled in wine and a little thereof held in the mouth eases the pain of toothache." Pliny wrote: "It is good to fasten loose teeth, and the juice of the root, mingled with honey, is good for weak eyes. Juice of the leaves and a little vinegar mixed together procures rest and sleep."

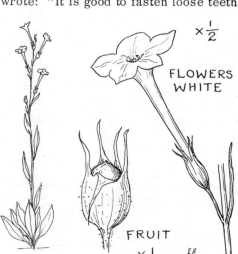

$\times \frac{1}{2}$

FLOWERS
WHITE

FRUIT
$\times$ 1   ER

H-46. INDIAN TOBACCO, <u>Nicotiana</u> sp. (<u>N.</u> <u>bigelovii</u>, Indian Tobacco, illustrated). 1-5' tall herbs (except 1 shrub with yellow flowers, <u>N.</u> <u>glauca</u>), with strong-scented, narcotic-poisonous leaves, and large white or greenish-white flowers.

SW
Clt.
Oak

Most
Sts.

In early days the leaves were used for ailments of the chest and lungs by making a syrup in distilled water. A tobacco leaf was applied to the head to relieve pains and migrain. Seeds eased pains of toothache and leaves were burned for ashes and used as a tooth-powder. Distilled juice put in cuts, sores and old wounds, promoted healing. Indians gathered the whole plant when seeds were ripe but leaves still green.   They dried and crumbled the leaves for smoking. A mixture of different leaves was used with the tobacco, such as bear berry and sumac, also the bark of dogwood scraped. Indian women smoked tobacco only to cure colds. A decoction of powdered leaves was drunk as an effective emetic (to cause vomiting). The plant is reported to be poisonous to stock.

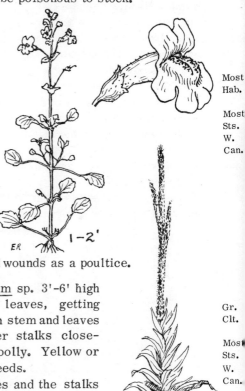

H-47. MONKEY FLOW-ERS, Mimulus sp., Figwort Fam. (M. guttatus, Common Monkey Flower, illustrated). Generally herbs with opposite leaves; the flower 2-lipped and yellow, purple, red or violet, with the throat open or closed by a palate (obstruction); usually plants are 1-2' tall.

Indians used both young stems and leaves for salad greens. Root of Yellow Mimulus used as astringent. Raw leaves and stems were applied when crushed to rope burns and wounds as a poultice.

Most Hab.

Most Sts. W. Can.

H-48. MULLEIN, Verbascum sp. 3'-6' high herbs, with long, oval, basal leaves, getting smaller toward top of stem; both stem and leaves generally very woolly. Flower stalks close-packed, 1-3' high, also very woolly. Yellow or white flowers produce brown seeds.

In early days the downy leaves and the stalks were dipped in grease and used for candle and lamp wicks. Dioscorides said: "A small quantity of decoction of roots given for cramps and convulsions, and, likewise, those troubled with

Gr. Clt.

Most Sts. W. Can.

old coughs; eases toothache." He also suggested mixing seeds and flowers with flowers of Camomile and powder of dry Venice turpentine to throw on coals in a chafing dish, producing warm fumes, that, kept in a closed container, gave relief to piles. And he said 3 ounces of the distilled water of the flowers drunk morning and evening, was a good remedy for gout.

Indians dried leaves and smoked them to relieve lung troubles. Mullein also has astringent properties, being used for bleeding of the lungs; while flower oil was used for earache and coughs.

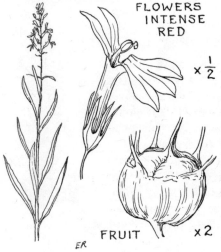

FLOWERS BLUE

x1

x1

10"-18"   ER   FRUIT

FLOWERS INTENSE RED

x ½

ER   FRUIT   x2

H-49. PENSTEMON, Penstemon sp. (P. gracilentus, Slender Penstemon, (illustrated). Very numerous species, mostly herbs, but a few shrubs (see p. 30); noted for long tube-like, showy flowers, red, blue, purple, yellow or white in color; opposite leaves; flowers irregular.

Most Hab.

Most Sts. W. Can.

Spanish New Mexicans boil flowering tops and drink liquid for kidney trouble. Indians made a wash and a poultice for running sores; also steeped tops for colds. Red penstemons were boiled and the solution used as a wash for burns. It is said to stop pain and help new skin to grow.

SW Wtr.

Most Sts. W. Can.

H-50. LOBELIA, Lobelia sp., Bluebell Fam. (L. cardinalis, Scarlet Lobelia or Cardinal Flower, illustrated). 1-2' high herbs, with leafy-bracted, red, yellow, white or blue flowers, which are 2-lipped and highly irregular; leaves alternate.

Indians used the root and

plant of red Lobelia for syphilis and for expelling or destroying intestinal worms. An overdose acts as a narcotic. Milky juice of the plant is poisonous. It is a diaphoretic (increasing perspiration). Materia Medica suggests using the Blue Lobelia for prostration following influenza, and the Red Lobelia to help sticking pains in the chest on taking a long breath. The Shoshones made a tea of Lobelia for use as an emetic (to cause vomiting) and a physic.

H-51. MULE'S EARS, Wyethia sp., Sunflower Fam. Most Wyethia grow in dense clumps in fairly dry, open places, from 1'-3 1/2' tall; generally with 1 to few large, yellow (white in 1 species), flower heads; basal leaves usually quite large. In the Common Mountain Mule Ears, W. mollis, (illustrated), the foliage is white woolly when young, turning to greenish when older. Stock and deer eat the flowers.

Md.
Chap.
Oak
CCF
MCF

Indians used the roots as food, fermenting them on heated stones in the ground for 1 or 2 days. The flavor is sweet and agreeable. Roots were also used as a poultice for relief of pains and bruises. A decoction of leaves was used as a bath, producing profuse sweating. It should never be tak-

Most
Sts.
W.
Can.

en internally, as it is considered poisonous. Wyethia is listed in homeopathic medicines as used for pharyngitis (a throat irritation common among singers and speakers) and for hay fever.

Klamath Indians used the mashed roots as a poultice for swellings. Nevada Indians ground the resinous roots and soaked them in water to make a solution that was taken as an emetic (to induce vomiting). Often, for this purpose, they boiled the roots until the solution became quite concentrated. A combination remedy is to make a tea by boiling the chopped roots with the end twigs of the juniper (Juniperus utahensis), and take for colds and fevers.

H-52. ARROW-
LEAVED BALSAM-
ROOT, Balsamorhiza
sagittata. 8-26" high
herb, with tuft of
large basal leaves,
naked stems, few yel-
low flower heads, and
thick root. Contains
a volatile oil with tur-
pentine-like odor; re-
ported to be poison-
ous.

Most
Hab.

Most
Sts.
W.
Can.

Important forage
plant. Indians win-
nowed and cracked
the seeds as food.
The root was peeled,
boiled and ground;
then cooled and drunk
for rheumatism or
headache. A small
cupful was taken for rheumatism and patient covered as the drug
caused profuse perspiration. The mashed root or the dry, powdered root was applied as
a dressing for syphlitic
sores; also mashed root
used for swellings or in-
sect bites. The gummy
root sap was swallowed
for consumption.

RAY FLOWERS
YELLOW

DISK
FLOWERS
BROWN

Most
Hab.

Most
Sts.
W.
Can.

× 1/2

2'- 5'

ER

H-53. COMMON SUN
FLOWER, Helianthus an-
nuus. The coarse, many-
branched, rough stems
grow 3'-6' tall; leaves
about 6" long; large yel-
low flower heads.

Roasted seeds are good
to eat. Spanish used the

seeds to make a meal or gruel.   Indians capitalized upon the
seed oil to grease their hair, boiling the flower heads to get it.
Roots were used in combination with other roots for snake bite,
and a root decoction was used as a warm wash for rheumatism.
A purple and black dye was extracted from seeds for clothes and
baskets; also a yellow dye was derived from the plant.   Roasted
seeds or shells crushed and sifted were used as a drink like coffee.   Ripe seeds parched and made into a meal or bread is very
nutritious.   Stalks yield a fibre.

Pharmacopia says, "Seed diuretic, yields a blond fixing oil; the
plant is anti-malarial." Bees make a fine, amber honey from the
flowers. Sun flower oil is fed to sheep, cattle and poultry; claimed
to be better than linseed oil.

H-54.   GRINDELIA, GUM PLANT,
RESIN WEED, Grindelia sp.   Usually
1'-6' high herbs, rather resinous, especially around the flowers; single or
branched stems; rather stiff pointed
leaves with toothed edges; large yellow
flowers solitary or few in cluster.

Brooks Botany says: "Root in Spring
dried and powdered, makes a fine medicine for purging or hemorrhages. The
decoction of the whole plant is famous
for wounds and, in England, it was used
for ulcers." Spanish Americans boiled
buds and flowers until water was down
to a pint, then that was drunk for kidney trouble. For rheumatism,
fresh plant was crushed and applied to body part. Official use of
drug: fluid extract made from flowering top and leaves, a stomach tonic, anti-spasmodic; also, fluid extract painted on surfaces
affords relief to those suffering from ivy or oak poisoning.

Msh
Sage
Clt.
Gr.

Most
Sts.

Indians boiled root and drank tea for the liver; buds on the plant
were dried for use with small-pox; a decoction of leaves was made
for running sores; flowering tops, collected in the spring, were
used for a blood purifier and to relieve throat and lung trouble; a
small quantity of decoction held in the mouth, but never swallowed,
helped to cure toothache. Small dosages of a decoction of the plant
were taken each day for small pox, also a half cupful a day for
measles.   A half cupful hot was said to be good for pneumonia.

FLOWERS YELLOW

H-55.   GOLDENROD,
Solidago sp. 1-7' high herbs,
with usually simple stems
rising from a woody base or
underground stem. The
small, yellow flower heads
are in panicles, racemes
and cymes. S. californica,
the California Goldenrod, is
very common in California
fields (illustrated). Stems
usually densely leafy.

Md.
Gr.
Clt.
Oak
CCF
MCF

Most
Sts.
W.
Can.

Indians boiled leaves and
used decoction to wash on
wounds and ulcers, then
sprinkled powdered leaves on wounds. The same remedy was
used for saddle sores on horses. A yellow dye was made. Spanish Americans used the fresh plant mixed with soap for a plaster
to bind on sore throats. Pharmacopia says it is astringent, diaphoretic (increasing prespiration), and used for cleansing sores.

The Missouri Goldenrod, S. missouriensis (of Br. Columbia,
Oregon and east), told by its unusually long-stemmed and fluted
leaves), had the leaves eaten as a salad.

H-56. WESTERN MUGWORT, Artemisia ludoviciana. Slender to moderately stout
herb, 1'-5' tall; small,
yellow to purplish and
hairy flowers, in dense
spikes; numerous leaves
are densely white woolly;
generally in shady spots.

FLOWER HEAD

Sage
MCF
Gr.
Oak

Most
Sts.
W.
Can.

Dioscorides says:
"Dissolves gallstones.
Juice made with myrrh
works with same effect as
do the roots; also being
made up with axungia (hog
or goose grease) into an
ointment, takes away wens
and hard knots."

"Three drams of the powder of dried leaves taken in wine is a speedy and best cure for sciatica (a painful affliction of the hip)." Pliny says: "If a traveler bind some of the herb about him, he will feel no weariness on his journey."

Indians used it medicinally by making a decoction of the leaves for colds, colic, bonchitis, rheumatism and fever. A poultice was made for wounds, and the juice was used for poison oak. A leaf inserted in one nostril was supposed to cure headache.

H-57. COMMON YARROW or MILFOIL, <u>Achillea</u> <u>millefolium</u>. A fairly showy plant, 1-3' high, on long stems with finely-divided leaves and flat-topped, white flower clusters (rarely yellow); foliage appears grayish from numerous tiny hairs.

Leaves reported to stop bleeding of wounds and to heal inflamation. Powdered, dry herb taken with Plantain water, will halt internal bleeding and juice put in the eye will take away redness (says Achilles). Oil made from the plant stops falling hair.

The Indians picked and dried the whole plant. They put a handful of the dried material in a small amount of boiling water and used as a tonic for rundown conditions and indigestion. The leaves were used as a poultice for rash.

Most Hab.

Most Sts. W. Can.

H-58. CUDWEED or EVERLASTING FLOWER, <u>Gnaphalium</u> sp. (<u>G</u>. <u>palustre</u>, Lowland Cudweed, illustrated). 4-36" tall herbs with aromatic scent and usually woolly leaves. Small, white, yellow, purplish or

SW
Oak
CCF
MCF
Chap

Most
Sts.

reddish flowers; flowers have numerous rounded pearly heads on top of stems with woolly papery feeling. It is poor forage.

Indians used leaves for catarrhal infections and decoction of the leaves for intestinal and pulmonary catarrah (inflamation of membranes); also for bruises. The bruised plant assists in healing wounds, and an infusion (steeping leaves in cold water) is used for increasing perspiration.

H-59. COAST TARWEED, Madia sativa. 1 1/2'-3' tall, aromatic, glandular herb, with large, yellow or white flower heads; stout stem rigidly branched.

Gr.
Clt.

Was.
Ore.
Cal.
W.
Can.

The oil expressed from the seed is made into cake for cattle feed. It is also a good table oil and a lubricant. The oily content of the seed is very nutritious and the Indians would gather them in summer and grind into a fine meal to be eaten dry. They also scalded the seeds, yielding an oil used in soap making. For their medicine, flowering tops were a poison oak remedy and a tonic of the leaves was reported useful in treatment of inflammatory rheumatism. Northern California Indians made a cough syrup by drying the buds.

SW
Oak
MCF
CCF
Clt.
PJ

Was.
Id.
Ore.
Cal.
Nev.
Ut.
N. M.
Ar.

H-60. COMMON THOROUGHWORT or BONESET, Eupatorium sp. 1'-4' tall herbs, with hairy branches at top; flowers in nodding groups of heads or flat-topped clusters, white, pink or red; no ray flowers; leaves mainly opposite, especially in white-flowered species.

Flowering tops gathered in full bloom and stripped from stalk, are dried and kept to make into bitter tonic or tea. Tonic is cathartic and emetic (causing vomiting). The tea is taken cold as a tonic; a hot infusion is used for malarial fever. Indians called it Ague Plant due to its malarial healing quality.

SUGGESTED REFERENCES

Angier, Bradford. LIVING OFF THE COUNTRY; the Stackpole Company, 1956.

Bell, J. W. NATURE'S REMEDIES, A Practical Manual for the Curative Power of Herbs; Chas. T. Branford Co., 1958. Covers several common weeds found in the United States.

Fernald, Merritt L. and Alfred Charles Kinsey; Revised by Reed C. Rollins. EDIBLE WILD PLANTS OF EASTERN NORTH AMERICA; Harper and Brothers, 1958. This book describes mainly eastern plants, but has in it a number of species also found in the west.

Jaeger, Ellsworth. WILDWOOD WISDOM; the Macmillan Company, 1961. Very complete.

INDEX OF PLANTS

64